MW01107614

The Batter's Edge

The Batter's Edge

A Year With The Boston Red Sox

Scott D. Olivieri

iUniverse, Inc.

New York Lincoln Shanghai

The Batter's Edge
A Year With The Boston Red Sox

All Rights Reserved © 2003 by Scott D. Olivieri

No part of this book may be reproduced or transmitted in any form or by any means, graphic, electronic, or mechanical, including photocopying, recording, taping, or by any information storage retrieval system, without the written permission of the publisher.

iUniverse, Inc.

For information address:
iUniverse, Inc.
2021 Pine Lake Road, Suite 100
Lincoln, NE 68512
www.iuniverse.com

ISBN: 0-595-29563-0

Printed in the United States of America

for Kate and my parents, Pete and Rita, with gratitude

Contents

1

A Believer

I am a child of the Boston Red Sox. Therefore, I am a historian, a pessimist, and I dwell on details. I know what can go wrong because I've seen it before, or read about it, or been schooled by relatives.

As I was raised on the Red Sox, my mind collected details like a lint brush and there was always room for more. There are mounds of names and dates and numbers in my head—Paxton, Jurak, Goodman, Dropo, 1918, .406, $11^{1/2}$—details about players no one's ever heard of, specifics of games that didn't matter. It all adds up to a whole lot of stuff I can't really use. For example, I've always known the years the Red Sox made the playoffs since 1918: '46, ('48), '67, '75, ('78), '86 ('88 and '90 are unsightly blemishes, unworthy of mention), '95, '98, '99, '03. I can write down the starting lineup and each player's uniform number from every team since I was eight years old. When I was eleven, my older brother Kevin and I could recite the top ten hitters in the American League, rattling off every player's batting average within three percentage points. Were we fanatics? I don't think so. We were just like all the other kids we knew in eastern Massachusetts in the mid '70s.

Being a Red Sox fan was never just a hobby. Fan is an inappropriate term—it's flat and generic, and trivializes the commitment. It has this cavalier ring to it that belongs in Milwaukee or San Diego. *Member* is more accurate. Or disciple. Or believer. Believers have countless practical and educational benefits. Never in my life have I failed to remember a locker combination. Using uniform numbers as my code, eighth grade was Evans-Stapleton-Nichols (24-11-51); ninth grade was Stanley-Remy-Allenson (46-2-39). It was easy. Baseball was my geography lesson: I could spell Milwaukee and knew where it was because they had the Brewers and Robin Yount and Paul Molitor and Gorman Thomas. I knew Chicago was larger than Atlanta because they had two teams. Baseball taught me weather conditions, time zones and assorted tidbits of all major US cities: Kansas City is deathly humid in July, Minnesota is in the central time zone (first pitch at 8:35), and Texas has mosquitoes the size of moths. I also decided that states like Arkansas, Tennessee and Maine were useless because they did not have baseball teams. And with the misplaced pride of a stubborn 9-year-old, I remember mocking Mainers, though I had never met anyone from there. They were hockey-loving backwoodsmen feeding off our team, transients who wandered into Fenway a few times a year (during a winning streak) and pledged their allegiance. In reality, some of the more diehard and knowledgeable Red Sox fans come from northern New England, but I was just a loyal kid checking passports at the border of Red Sox Nation, protecting something I cherished and considered mine.

In the town of Winchester, your Little League jersey number was a springboard for imagination. It allowed you to step on a field in your town and be just like a Major League Baseball player. For a few hours each Saturday, you wore your shirt—his number—in front of fans (moms, dads, younger sisters), you stood up at-bat just like he did, you wore your hat like he did, you pounded your glove if he pounded his glove, you threw your helmet if he threw his helmet, and you spit like he spit. You wore your shirt, with attitude wherever you went: riding your bike, at the grocery store, getting on the bus. This probably wasn't true for everyone; I guess it depended on what number you had. My brother had number sixteen, worn by light-hitting reserve outfielder Rick Miller, so he dismissed it, never wore the jersey other than at games and practices. As a fifth grader in 1977, I was handed number fourteen. Rarely have the gods of chance smiled so broadly upon me, for in 1977 the Red Sox had a slugger by the name of Jim Rice who would explode over the next five years, terrorizing American League pitchers with a graceful swing and signature bat release. He and I wore the same number: therefore, some unwritten, obscure, but universally understood law of association connected me to this man. His home runs were, in some small way, my victories. My brother would cheer after another Jim Rice game-winning shot to left, but we both understood I could make a bit more noise, and was entitled to some additional measure of satisfaction. I wore his number.

My childhood passion for the Red Sox felt like a leech nestled in a hidden spot between my heart and armpit, capable of injecting adrenaline directly into my body during late inning comebacks, heroic defensive plays, or a bench-clearing brawl with the Yankees. The drugs would wear off, suddenly, without warning, as a Sox reliever self-destructed in the eighth, or Hobson threw wildly into the dugout. The leech would drift to my armpit, sting like razor burn, fill the day with the rancid odor of defeat, and leave me begging for relief. In the darkest hours of a child's overreaction ('78, '86, others) I would retreat to my room and mope in the dark like an addict scratching his eyes out for another hit of acid, listening to season highlight records of the '67 and '75 Red Sox teams and looking for a flicker of good news that could turn things around. O.K., maybe I'm overstating it, and it was never quite that dramatic; but the Red Sox are about hyperbole, about powerful teams with superb talent losing in ways screenwriters couldn't script, about a series of blunders committed by different players, decades apart, players with splendid mental and physical gifts, connected only by the uniform they wore and an untimely mistake. The Red Sox, ultimately, are a symbol of disappointment, and when that comes (as it always does) we anxiously await another chance, another season to stick it to the Yankees (or spank-me's, as we called them; I'm not sure why other than it was funny and somehow derogatory), another spring where we have a stronger roster and a lead in April.

The *Globe* and the *Herald* fed my appetite; all winter Gammons and McDonough conjectured about trades and possible free-agent signings. The stories were spread out over the cold months (usually they communicated next to nothing) and we devoured these fragments over a bowl of Frosted Flakes or a waffle and absorbed every word, X'ing in black marker each day that stood between December and the first day of spring training.

The major events of my life are attached to the team the Red Sox fielded that summer. As a small child unable to stay up past the 6th inning, I was sent to bed wondering if Petrocelli would go deep or Tiant would complete the shutout. I'd fall asleep to the radio voices of Ned Martin or Ken Coleman filling my room, vividly dictating the late-inning events in words clearer than television. After my First Communion, Steven Scali and I emulated infielders Rick Burleson and Denny Doyle; shuffling the ball back and forth a hundred times until we made the perfect ninth-inning, bases-loaded, one-out, up-by-a-run, game-saving double play. Our first baseman (the Schultzes' fence) always made the perfect scoop of a low throw just in time to nail the imaginary hustling runner.

During the heat wave of 1978, we retreated to the musty basement couch and watched the Red Sox crush balls into the stands. At the All-Star break we led the Yankees by eleven and a half games, then watched as our team fell apart, first physically, then emotionally, until the Sox rallied in the final week and earned the right to play the Yankees in a one-game playoff on an October Monday. On the way home from school, the bus driver told us the Sox had a 2-1 lead. As we rode up Dunster Lane, a bus full of kids who bickered every other day of the year chanted in a single voice, "Here we go Red Sox! Here we go!" Two hours later, when Yaz popped up to end the game, my father got up from his chair without a word, walked into the garage, and slammed the door. I could hear him banging his tools on something that probably didn't need fixing. My brother yelled, "Goddamned Yankees! I hate them!" I clenched my fist and wanted to punch the TV, but instead thought of the worst word I knew and said it twenty times in succession as the Yankee idiots rejoiced behind the third base bag. They hadn't won the World Series, but they'd just beaten the best team in baseball in their home park, so they knew the rest of the ride would be easy. Since that day, the name "Bucky Dent" has never been spoken in our house.

The summer I turned eleven, I knew I couldn't hit home runs like Jim Rice, but hoped I could steal bases like Jerry Remy or make diving catches like Fred Lynn. I made the All-Star team every year in Little League and was determined to play for the Boston Red Sox. In my first year of high school, I played solid defense and was an above average hitter, but the following year I lost the starting third-base job to David Alexander. There was a game early in the season—it was at Melrose—and we were down a few runs late in the game when the coach asked me to pinch-hit. I struck out on three pitches. Didn't even foul one off. As I stared out the window on the bus ride home, I realized I would never play for the Red Sox, or even be a varsity starter. At sixteen, my baseball career was over.

I couldn't fall asleep that night. A cool May breeze inflated the curtains while I listened to the post-game interview with pitcher Mark Clear, then Bob Starr's post-game summary and commentary. After your first dream dissolves, you change—suddenly, imperceptibly, permanently. As I lifted myself out of bed the next morning, I was a little less eager to begin the day, a little less anxious to read the box score, and a little less sure of who I was.

The Red Sox struggled throughout my high school years. They traded Hobson and Burleson, and lost Fisk because they failed to mail him his contract, which was due on my eleventh birthday. Most of their minor league talent of the early '80s never reached star quality, and the Sox languished in mediocrity as they transitioned into a team without Carl Yastrzemski.

Captain Carl *was* the Red Sox. Intense. Tough. A Yankee-hater. Yaz had a gravelly voice that made you believe everything he said. I had watched Yaz my entire life. I was born the year after he single-handedly led the Sox to the 1967 World Series, but Yaz's longevity enabled me to catch the second half of his brilliant career. As a first-grader, I watched him reel in balls from the left field wall as if they were yo-yo's returning to a magic finger. When I had a homework assignment in third grade to do a report on a leader, I chose Carl Yastrzemski. In the summer after seventh grade, we waited days for him to get his 3,000th hit, and an eternity for him to get his 400th home run. As his legs slowed and his back ached, I saw him move from left field to first base, then to DH. And when he retired, and I knew I'd never again see his cocked shoulder and upright bat reaching into the sky, it was as if my favorite uncle had died. The Sox stumbled for a few years trying to find a post-Yaz identity.

In the mid '80s, Wade Boggs came and slammed doubles off the wall in left; Roger Clemens arrived and blew hitters away with heaters. They brought with them the hope and youthful optimism Lynn and Rice had provided a decade earlier, but the two stars clashed. Veterans Dwight Evans, Jim Rice and Don Baylor kept them focused, and the team soon became a powerful force in the American League East. When I was in high school, I was sure they'd win it all during the next few years; they had tremendous hitters, solid pitching (which I had never seen in a Red Sox team before), and better than average defense. Their best chance was in 1986, when I was a freshman in college. Everyone's heard about it: the Red Sox were up by two runs in the bottom of the tenth inning, with no one on and two outs. They were one strike away from winning the World Series, but the gods of baseball did not cooperate. And don't give me that crap about Buckner, it wasn't just Buckner; it was Stanley and Gedman and Schiraldi—everyone was to blame. The Mets slapped three consecutive hits. Run scored. Then the Sox melted. Wild pitch. Run scored. Error. Run scored. Game over. For the first time in my life I hated the Red Sox, every single one of them.

Wade Boggs was there. When the Mets took game six of the World Series, I heard he raided the mini-bar in his hotel room, smashed the table lamp, and battered the phone with his fist. Boggs considered asking for a trade or even playing in Japan. Shrapnel from the '86 disaster plagued him for months in the form of headaches, numbness and tingling in his legs, and sudden shaking in his hands. He told me the emptiness in his chest never left him; he wanted to tear himself open and beat it out. Despite a winter of anger and despair, he returned to hit .363 the following season. When I told him I didn't see any of it, that I could only bring myself to watch three games during the entire 1987 season, he nodded.

"Not surprised," he said.

I wasn't there during the '86 debacle—I didn't pitch any innings or get a single at-bat—but I was a Red Sox believer, and Wade Boggs knew what that meant.

2

The Idea

It was my father's idea. I had no clue what was going on and
only became involved later, after he'd built the first prototype.
In 1991, I was lost in a post-college stupor. I hated my job,
loved my girlfriend, and felt compelled to buy a sports car I
couldn't afford. The job was as a computer assistant at New
England Sports Network, a cable television station covering
the Red Sox and Bruins (and table tennis); my girlfriend was
Kate, a girl I'd met a few months earlier at Boston College; the
car was a red 1986 Ford Mustang GT convertible.

My income tax forms would have told you I lived in my
parents' house in Winchester, but most of my clothes, my
computer, and my nineteen-inch color TV were at Kate's
apartment in nearby Woburn. During a rare evening at my
legal residence, I was eating a bowl of cereal, watching *Cheers*
reruns on the black-and-white TV in the kitchen when my
father sat down next to me.

"I need your help with something."

"What is it?"

When he did not reply, I turned to look at him.

"What?" I said through a mouthful of Apple Jacks.

"It's important." He reached to shut off the TV.

"Wait, it's almost over. Five minutes, I want to see what happens to Norm."

I raised the bowl, slurped the remaining milk, and when I put it down, he was gone. When the show was over (Norm started a painting business and hired a creepy secretary), I went looking for my father in the basement, then the garage. I found him upstairs in his office, typing at the computer.

A strange machine rested on the desk beside him. It was white and thicker than three phonebooks, with no model number or brand name on it, just a half-dozen red and gray buttons and a slot on the front large enough for a Frisbee.

"What the hell is that thing?" I said.

He pretended not to hear me.

I'd been around my dad for twenty-one years, yet failed to grasp his basic rules of interaction: when he needed me to do something (which was not very often), I had to drop what I was doing, follow him, and complete the task immediately. Otherwise, it was pure agony.

I approached the desk and looked over his shoulder. "Hmm what you got there, some code?"

Silence.

After standing behind him for several moments, I walked over to the window and looked out into the neighbor's yard, where I could see three young kids splashing in the Moda's swimming pool.

My father continued typing as I sat on the rust-colored recliner in the corner and scanned the jammed bookshelves along the far wall. *Computer Information Systems Analysis.*

HyperCard. The Macintosh Bible. Programmer's Guide. How does he read this stuff?

"This is it, Scott."

I shuddered to attention, like when my name is finally called at the Registry of Motor Vehicles.

A cable rested in the palm of his hand, his fingers gently holding it in place. His body was motionless, his head angled slightly to the left, studying the cable. Exposed red, white, and green wires twirled around each other, finally meeting at a silver adapter.

"A cable?"

"I made this," my father said.

"Congratulations."

He smirked, turned away. I don't know why he put up with me.

"So what is it?" I asked.

"You want to know, wiseacre?"

"Yes."

"It connects the Mac to this." He tapped his hand on the massive white thing.

"What, the pizza oven?"

He tried to look mad. "You're such a stiff!"

"Thanks."

"It's a laserdisc recorder, bozo."

"Huh?"

"A laserdisc recorder."

"What do you need *that* for?"

When he didn't answer, I rephrased my question. "What are you doing with it? Where'd you get it?"

"I'm borrowing it from someone I know at Panasonic."

"So what do you need me for?" I asked.

"Some grunt work."

"Super. I'm your guy. I have no marketable skills, so this is right up my alley."

"I need you to watch video on this monitor and type the counter numbers into the Mac."

"How long will it take?"

"A few hours."

"Okay, set me up."

He pressed the green PLAY button on the laserdisc machine, and video appeared on a small TV monitor just to the left of the Macintosh.

"The Sox game?" I turned in my chair to face him. "You want me to watch the Sox play Oakland?"

"Yes," he said, slightly irritated. "I want you to watch the Sox game."

"What the heck is this? What are you doing?"

"Just do what I tell you."

"Like the tool that I am, right?"

"See this button?" He pointed at a blue button with two vertical lines on it, the same symbol VCR's used to indicate PAUSE. "As the pitcher starts his windup, pause the video, then type the counter number from the laserdisc player into this field here on the Macintosh screen."

"Okay."

"After you get the counter number, press PLAY. When the catcher catches the ball, or the hitter puts the ball in play, press PAUSE again and write down the counter number. This will let the computer know exactly where the video of that at-bat is located."

"Sure, sounds easy enough. How many of these at-bats should I do?"

"As many as you can. I'll check back."

This was nothing new; my father had been giving me petty technical tasks as long as I can remember. When I was in fifth grade we had this big contraption that was some kind of basic computer. I don't really remember what it was used for, but he would plug in the cables in a certain order and the lights would flash, or remain steady, or make some kind of pattern, depending on how it was wired. Sometimes he'd ask me to arrange the circuits in a certain order, then he'd leave the room. My friends had to mow the lawn or take out the garbage; I did electrical engineering.

Whenever I needed money and asked for a job, he'd give me something to do on the computer. In grade school, I'd use this old Digital word processor that was larger than a refrigerator to format and print his magazine articles. When I was in junior high, I'd clean out some disks for him on our Apple II for cash, and in high school, I'd enter data into HyperCard records on the Macintosh. I was a menial computer task mercenary.

My father knew computers were the future. His tactics were remarkable if not covert: give the kids technical work to get them ahead of their peers, spark an interest in computers, and set them up for the future. For all his efforts, I majored in English Literature.

So here I was, graduated from college, of legal drinking age, and holding down a full-time job, yet still doing computer work for my dad. But this was different, and from the moment I sat down at the desk, I could sense something magical about how these two devices worked together.

I neglected my assignment and went into exploratory mode, randomly pressing buttons on the laserdisc machine. Pressing any button caused the device to beep. I played video, paused it, and brought up a menu with dozens of choices. Suddenly, the machine beeped three times and churned for a few seconds before spitting out a thick white cartridge. *Oops, I guess that white button was eject. Couldn't they afford to put labels on this thing?* I pulled the disc out and inspected it. It was heavy and had a sliding panel on it similar to a floppy disk except it was silver. When I slid it open, it revealed a CD the size of a dinner plate.

Damn, that's cool.

"Getting a lot done?"

My father was standing in the doorway, his legs crossed, arms folded. I felt like I had been caught experimenting with his power tools.

"Hey, this thing is really something."

"Glad you like it. How much did you get done?"

"Basically nothing."

"Okay, so what can you tell me?"

"The laserdiscs have 54,000 frames. Kind of a weird number, huh?"

He grinned.

"And they don't hold a heck of a lot of video. I flipped to the end of the disc and *Dopson* was still in the game. That guy's always getting hammered—he'll go four innings, five if he's lucky—so that means the disc only holds about ninety minutes of the game."

"Not even. Did you see any commercials? What about all the dead time in between pitches?"

"That's right–"

"I cut it all out."

"How many minutes do they hold?"

"Thirty."

"That's it? That's nothin'. Couldn't you just get another disc?"

"They're prohibitively expensive."

"How much?"

"A thousand dollars."

"Each? For one disc?" I stood up.

He nodded.

"Holy crap! You're kiddin' me!"

He wasn't.

"What else can you tell me?"

"Ummm, the discs are shiny."

My father stared blankly back at me.

"I didn't get a chance to mess around with the computer."

"Let me show you."

He leaned over my shoulder and mouse-clicked a few times on the computer screen. A grid appeared, with the name, "Wade Boggs," at the top. He pressed a few buttons on the laserdisc, then stood back from the table.

"Start clicking, let's see what happens."

I slapped my hand on the mouse and clicked wildly on the screen. An error message appeared, then the program closed.

"What are you doing?" my father asked.

"I just–"

"I asked you to try it out, not beat on it!"

"But I–"

"I just started creating the program, it's not ready for you, foolishly clicking all over the screen."

He put his right hand on top of mine. I cringed, withdrew my arm, and forfeited control of the mouse.

He brushed my shoulder with the back of his hand. "Up, up."

"Evicted."

"Yes, you've been evicted."

My father took a deep breath and launched the program. "I've written a Panasonic video driver that enables the computer to send commands to the laserdisc player." I didn't understand or care what this meant, but I endured his perfunctory technical overview. "Using the computer, you can jump around the laserdisc and show any video segment you'd like."

"I monkeyed around with the laserdisc. I could type in a number on the small keypad on the laserdisc player and the video on the laserdisc at that number would appear on the TV monitor."

"But what good is that if you have to type in all these numbers?" he asked.

"That's no good."

"You'd have to keep a list of all the counter numbers and then type them in when you wanted to see a certain segment of video. But then someone like you would screw it up or lose the numbers."

"Thanks, I appreciate it."

"No one wants to write down all these numbers, or type them in."

"That would be a hassle," I said.

"It was difficult to overcome this hurdle. I was stumped for months."

"Months! How long have you been working on this? Why didn't you tell me?"

"I don't need to tell you everything."

I clicked my tongue in disapproval.

"Nevertheless, I was stumped. I decided to let the Macintosh remember the counter numbers for me. I wrote this HyperCard program to store all the counter numbers, and then I made a user interface that people can use to control it."

"Geez, sounds like a lot of work."

"It was."

We turned our attention to the computer screen, which contained four numbered buttons, each representing an at-bat for Wade Boggs during this particular game against the A's. My father clicked the button labeled "one" to view his first at-bat. Suddenly, video flashed on the TV monitor beside the computer, and I saw Dave Stewart throwing a pitch to Boggs. He threw another pitch, then a third, which Boggs lined into center for a single. The video stopped.

"O.K., so that was Boggs' first at-bat of the night. See how it's dusk? Now watch this!"

He clicked on the button labeled "three." The TV monitor went black for a moment and the laserdisc player hummed for two seconds before flashing up a video: it was still Stewart pitching to Boggs, but the sky was darker, the lights were on, and there was a runner on second. This time Boggs walked.

"This at-bat was more than *two hours* after his first at-bat, yet we can instantly access it, just like songs on an audio CD."

It was astonishing.

"How does it do that?"

I stood up and looked behind the computer, like Dorothy searching behind the curtain to demystify the wizard. "O.K., so that special cable you showed me goes from the computer to the laserdisc player, and it tells the laserdisc which video frames to play."

"You got it!" My father continued, "Sure, we could have a good old videotape of Boggs and put it in every time he comes up to bat."

"Yeah, wouldn't that be good enough?" I asked.

"But what happens two months from now when he wants to see all of his at-bats against Dave Stewart?"

"He'd have to search through the tape of that game to find it."

"And what happens when he has three different games against Stewart? These guys get six hundred at-bats a year; that's a lot of videotapes, a lot of fast forwarding. It's unmanageable."

"Well, then he's spending half the day searching through tapes instead of taking extra batting practice."

"Actually, he doesn't search for his own video, some other guy does it."

"They have a guy who just does videotapes?"

"Part-time. Some high school kid who does it when he's not picking up dirty towels."

"How do you know this?"

"I've been doing research."

"So you're designing this system for the towel video guy."

He shook his head. "He's never going to use it."

"Then why bother?"

"Because, with any luck you're gonna be the new video guy."

I looked at him for clues, but when it came to reading my father's expressions, I was illiterate. All I could see was the reflection of the computer screen in his glasses.

"Sure, good one," I said.

"Nothing's certain yet, of course. They haven't even seen it."

"Who hasn't seen it?"

"The Red Sox."

He stepped back from the table, and I swiveled in the chair to maintain eye contact.

"You're serious." *There's no way he could be serious.*

He raised his eyebrows slightly and nodded his head twice.

"So you…" I cleared my throat. "So, is there some meeting planned?"

"In a few weeks…at Fenway Park."

"You're out of your mind."

"Does that mean you don't want to attend?"

"Why do you need me? You can do it."

"What if they like it? I'm not about to quit my job for this. It's just a fun project."

"There's no way," I said. Then turning to him, "Do you think this could work? Do you think they'll like it?"

"They'd better. I've spent too much damn time on this!"

I stayed up until 4:00 A.M. entering the counter numbers for every pitch on the laserdisc. That was the easy part. Waiting three weeks for the meeting at Fenway Park was much more difficult.

3

The Red Sox Brass

My father stopped the car at the corner of Yawkey Way and Brookline Avenue, popped the trunk, and flipped the hazards. He peered at me through the side mirror as I lifted the three cases out of the trunk and placed them gently on the sidewalk. I waited by the equipment while he slipped the car on to Brookline Avenue and searched for a parking spot.

Hours before the first pitch, throngs of fans congregated on Yawkey Way. In a city plagued with racial tension, Fenway's bordering passageways and side streets comprised a rare area in Boston where you could observe pinstriped executives rubbing elbows with college students in torn jeans, Latinos draped with saucer-sized medallions passing elderly couples walking hand-in-hand, or wealthy entrepreneurs leaning out limousine windows bargaining with African-American men for front row seats.

On game day, drivers within four blocks of Fenway idled helplessly; pedestrians owned the streets because vendors owned the sidewalks. The air was filled with the smell of cheap cigars and thick Boston accents squawking orders at passersby:

"Get your programs here!"

"Peanuts! Get your peanuts!"

"Italian sausages!"

More often than not, newcomers stopped, acquiesced to these demands, and handed over four dollars in return for overcooked meat by-products, soaked in grease and covered with soggy frozen vegetables.

Yawkey Way was where the buzz began, where the pre-game energy simmered and stewed. The street hummed with the chatter of endless possibility: Would Clemens strike out fifteen? Would Boggs go 4-for-4? On this street, in this city, for just a few hours, past failures were forgotten and fresh starts were cultivated. The Sox were playing tonight—anything could happen.

Kate and I spent many evenings on Yawkey Way, leaning against the tired bricks of Fenway, gnawing sausages and observing the activity. Clusters of people slashed forward like schools of fish intersecting from opposite directions. Kids from Boston Latin High School or Northeastern University slid through, their eyes transfixed on some imaginary point beyond, pretending not to see people a few feet in front of them; fathers with young sons in tow plodded through the pack, hoping for a measure of courtesy, instead getting bumped and nudged in all directions. Kate and I blended various techniques, often practicing the "weave with indifference" method, but adding a vigilant peripheral eye to avoid a confused tourist or a disoriented drunk. Most of the time, we came early to avoid the headache.

It was just after nine on Monday morning and the team was in Detroit, so Yawkey Way was empty. Without the clutter and commotion to guide me, I nearly got lost walking down this grubby one-way street. A third of the way down, we found the entrance to the executive offices, an arrogant door of cherry-finished hardwood, belittling the aging bricks of the stadium's outer walls surrounding it on three sides. Sunlight sliced through the buildings. The early summer heat found me, settling on my face, sliding down my shirt collar. It dried up my throat and moistened by palms. The sun was only partially responsible; I was scared shitless I'd blow the opportunity of a lifetime.

A security guard inspected us as we approached. When we told him our business, he nodded once, crossed our name off a list, returned the clipboard to the table in front of him, and without a word pointed us up the stairs behind him, where Helen Robinson, the four-hundred-year-old receptionist, fielded three phone calls before addressing us.

"Why are you here?" she barked.

"We have a meeting with–"

"Name?"

I looked at my father. "Was it Furbeck?"

"No! Tell me your name!"

"I'm Peter Olivieri. This is–"

"Wait there," she said, pointing a scraggly finger at the brown couch against the wall.

"But we need to set up for our meeting," I said.

"Sit down." Then, turning her back to us, she said, "I'll tell you when you can go in."

Thirty-five minutes later we were led down a narrow hallway to the Red Sox executive offices, where we set up the equipment on a glossy table in a conference room on the second floor overlooking the field. My father had come to know a kind man named Jim Healey, who thought the idea was worth a shot and had persuaded the management team to listen to our presentation. He told us to be ready to go at ten o'clock. We were finished setting up with five minutes to spare. Our hosts were not as punctual.

Fifty minutes later, two men in dark blue suits entered the room. We weren't told who would be in attendance. (Perhaps it violated some secret policy.) The first, who introduced himself as Robert Furbush, wore black-rimmed glasses and a wool tweed coat. Shaking his hand was like pulling a two-by-four from the lumber pile at Home Depot. Behind him was an olive-skinned, balding man with a slick forehead who introduced himself as Jeff. Before shaking my hand, he raised his eyebrows, looked me up and down, and creased his lips in a haughty grin that made me want to kick him in the teeth.

Our hosts sat shoulder-to-shoulder, and Jeff spoke quietly, funneling his remarks directly into Furbush's ear. They were apparently discussing something important and confidential. (If nothing else, the Red Sox were cloaked in secrecy.) For fifteen minutes, we watched them whispering like junior high school girls, studying their fingernails, then examining, buffing, and adjusting their watches. Unwilling to emulate them, not brazen enough to initiate small talk, and unsure whether to look at them or the wall or the table, we cowered into our leather chairs and waited for the meeting to begin.

It began when General Manager Lou Gorman rumbled down the hall, pulled open the door, and squeezed into the room. For all that was written about him in the papers, I had expected an air of mystique about him, but his presence was decidedly mundane. He carried no aura, just seventy-five extra pounds and a grandfatherly blend of Old Spice and talcum powder. Beneath a pinstriped Armani dress shirt the size of a tablecloth, his chest heaved in reaction to the journey from his corner office down the hall. He smothered my hand in both of his, looked me in the eye, and bobbed his head several dozen times.

"Lou Gorman. Pleased to meet you." His fleshy cheeks and turkey neck jiggled with each nod before drooping back into place.

Over the course of the last three weeks, we had written a simple computer program that displayed Wade Boggs' at-bats against Oakland's Dave Stewart. Each at-bat was listed in a column, each pitch in a row. Unfortunately, we were unable to decipher the various types of pitches, so all we could fill in was the pitch location. When we were done, the screen looked something like this:

Wade Boggs vs. Dave Stewart

At-bat #1

pitch 1: low—strike

pitch 2: low—foul

pitch 3: middle—double

At-bat #2

pitch 1: inside—ball

pitch 2: inside—fly out

I was somewhat ashamed to be presenting Red Sox officials with such novice baseball analysis, but we had no alternative (I would later learn that Furbush, Jeff, and Lou couldn't tell a fastball from a slider, or a fastball from a beachball, for that matter). In the demonstration, we simply ran through the prototype; we used the computer mouse (which Lou and Furbush took special note of, as if they'd never used one before) to click on the description of each pitch and watched as the video segment flashed instantly on the television monitor. A click of the mouse then took us to video of an at-bat that may have been three innings later.

"As you can see, the system, which we call 'The Batter's Edge' saves constant rewinding and fast-forwarding," my father explained. Even with their self-important postures and limited remarks, I could sense they hadn't seen anything like it before.

"And when you're using a computer in this fashion, you can, of course, also use it to tally the number of pitches, or curveballs, or any type of data...but we're not the baseball experts. We'd need some input and assistance from some players and coaches to know what type of information would be valuable to gather."

They had no idea what he was talking about, and I was impressed that my father was perceptive enough to truncate his sentences when it was evident they either didn't understand or weren't interested. The Red Sox "brass," as they were called, left suddenly, as if the baseball world was on fire and required attention. Or maybe it was lunchtime. Only Lou shook my hand before leaving.

For a few minutes, we cleaned up in silence, powering down machines, opening cases, pulling plugs, and rolling cables.

"Dad, I think we sold 'em."

"Hmm. I'm not certain. I wish they had been more communicative."

I snorted a laugh. "Yeah, that Furbush guy wasn't exactly Mr. Congeniality, was he?"

"I'm afraid not."

"What a stiff. And what about that greeting? I've met frogs that were more cordial."

He put a finger to his lips. "Shh! Someone could hear us!"

"Sorry, I forgot. They probably have the whole place bugged. They're worse than the friggin' FBI."

As we waited for the elevator, Jeff strutted down the hall and looked me straight in the eye. I bobbed my chin to acknowledge him, then smiled.

"Hello, Jeff."

He looked down at the dark red carpet and brushed past me. As the elevator door closed us in, I turned to face my father. "Did you see that?"

"Perhaps they have stressful working conditions."

I smirked in defiance.

4

Inside the Vault

I spun through the Yawkey Way turnstile just after nine o'clock, proudly flashing my brand new identification badge to the officer standing watch. I remember the musty smell of the concourse as I entered through the employee gate for the first time.

On game day, Fenway was a crowded brick kiln that heated up as the innings progressed, baking fans in the stale heat as the teams sparred through the middle three, then boiled to a climax in the late innings as the beer kicked in and pinch hitters battled against bullpen specialists. But now the team was on the West Coast for ten days, so the park was deserted. Fenway was peaceful, stately.

A security guard held his ground—arms extended, palms up—as an elderly couple pleaded for admittance to snap a quick photo of the Green Wall. "One minute, that's all," the woman begged. A heavyset man in crumply pants sprayed the front of a beer stand with water, then watched the suds disappear into small rusted grates on the cement floor of the concourse. Those grates were the first of thousands of details I'd never noticed until Fenway Park became my place of business, and it is through these details that this cranky, dilapidated structure became redefined in my mind.

I twisted the solid steel handle to the Red Sox clubhouse, pulled on it sharply, and nearly tore my arm from the socket. *Damn, that's heavy.* I let the door shut, shook the discomfort from my arm, then glanced behind me to check for witnesses. The hundreds of times I subsequently opened the door, I pressed my right foot into the yellowed concrete, grabbed the handle in my right palm, measured the resistance, and leaned back slowly with all my weight, doing my best to make it look easy. I can still feel the drag of that door on sticky August mornings, or at 3:00 A.M. with nine beers in me after coming home from the West Coast, or in the chill of a September morning. The door was a quick reminder of where I was headed. Each time I opened it, I knew I was entering an exclusive club; I was an insider. And the last time I heard that door slam behind me, I knew I was a stranger, immediately, irrevocably. All the stories and gossip I heard, all the baseball knowledge I had, all the people I lived with and the personal details I knew had been updated for the last time. I was just another fan. And as players got older and careers ended, and as friends were traded or released, my connections to those behind the door evaporated. But on this May morning everything was just beginning.

A short hall led to a second steel door; I held it open and peered into the clubhouse. Daylight from Van Ness Street glowed from a row of small opaque windows, set high on the wall and covered with steel grates. Dozens of long, fluorescent bulbs housed in rusted casings flooded the room with an artificial white light that demanded the plush red carpets be freshly vacuumed.

Seated at a gray table in the center of the clubhouse was a man reading the *Boston Herald*, a cup of coffee resting on the table in front of him. As I stepped into the room, there was a crash behind me. I quivered, turned a shoulder toward the door, as if to blame it. The man seated at the table turned the page of his newspaper. I stood frozen in my tracks, uncertain what to do.

Navy blue batting helmets lined the right wall in neat rows. The freshly-laundered, wedding-gown white jerseys hanging in every locker were resplendent in the morning calm of the clubhouse. A pile of plush cotton towels dreaded their daily transformation from fragrant and fluffy to putrid and muddy. Then I saw it. *There's number 21! That's Clemens' locker.* Taped to the top of his locker were baseball cards of Jim Rice and Dwight Evans.

The man at the table lowered the newspaper and furrowed his brow in my direction. "You must be the new tape guy," he said.

I approached him, extending my hand. "Not exactly. I'm the new computer video analyst. It's a new position. But anyway, I am new and, well, I'm Scott Olivieri. Are you Fitzy?"

"Name's Joe." His limp fingers slipped away before I had the chance to accept them. "Fitzy told me you'd be coming."

"This place is great," I said. "So this is where the action is?"

He bit the cuticle of his index finger. I looked back at the door, pointing to it with my thumb. "Geez, that thing is like a darn bank vault, huh?"

Joe raised the newspaper enough to cover his face, effectively leaving the room. I wanted to disappear, then reenter, this time with a perfectly scripted first interaction. The phone mercifully intervened, but Joe let it ring until it stopped.

"Do you know where I'm going to be set up?"

Joe leaned back just enough to remove his feet from the table and then stood up gingerly, as if his entire body was sunburned. He pressed the coffee cup to his chapped lips for a final taste.

"Here," he said, waving an arm forward.

He took a deep breath, triggering a prolonged smoker's cough that continued as we mazed through a washroom, down a short hall, past the trainer's area, and into the weight room.

Pointing past the weight machines, he said, "Back there, that's The Cave."

Hidden deep in the belly of the clubhouse, no one—not other Red Sox employees, not media, not even celebrated *Boston Globe* columnist and ESPN Analyst Peter Gammons—was ever allowed access to The Cave. There wasn't much to it, just a table crowded with the boxed equipment we'd ordered (three monitors, two computers, a laserdisc player, and a printer), but it was private, which soon made it a close second to the toilet on the player popularity list.

I sorted through the boxes and wires, pulled out Styrofoam corners, removed protective plastic, and read manuals. Just after one o'clock I walked across the street, picked up a meatball sub at The Batter's Box on the other side of Yawkey and brought it back to the clubhouse. Joe's invoices from Russell

Athletic were spread all over the gray table, so I pulled out the chair in front of Tony Pena's locker and sat down to eat. On the wall above the soda dispenser was a framed black-and-white photograph of Ted Williams standing on the top step of the dugout.

Last week Lansdowne Street had been renamed Williams Way. It was mind-boggling to think that Ted Williams resided within these walls before and after his home games. *Which locker was his? Where did he sit after that doubleheader in 1941, when he went 6-for-8 and finished the season at .406? Did they hold his locker for him when he left to fly planes in World War II, then Korea?* I looked over my shoulder, then left, right, hoping his locker would jump out at me, but it didn't. Joe was within earshot, but I was afraid to bother him.

The lockers weren't like those at Winchester High— orange, too thin to stick your head in, with vents at the top and a standard combination lock—no, these were open, over-sized storage areas. Wade Boggs had eight boxes of Nike spikes lining the floor of his locker. Across the top of each locker was a three-inch wide black metal strip, which spelled out the player's name in thin, white magnetic letters. No permanent nameplates (the team was too cheap to buy them), and it was good thing because in a few years, Dan Duquette would storm in and shuffle players on and off the roster like it was a YMCA pickup basketball game.

A few locker nameplates held the imprints of veteran stars. The black strips had faded under years of exposure to neon bulbs, yet remained dark where the magnetic letters had been. I approached a locker adjacent to the manager's office. Three letters, "Y A Z", were hidden behind the name of the current occupant, ROMINE, a utility player who would use the locker for a few more weeks before being released. Players noticed the weathered plates, but they would never have asked to have the nameplates cleaned or replaced. Baseball culture is nothing if not respectful of its past; veteran players understand the outrageous salaries they earn were handed to them by the players of the '70s and '80s who fought for free agency, battled through strikes and collusion, and made sacrifices for the those who would fill their shoes. During my time in the clubhouse, I never saw Joe buff away the letters of an old name or heard him mention replacing the steel strips. Perhaps he left them as a reminder that Rice, Fisk, and Yaz were not names to be wiped away, or maybe he didn't even notice those old names—Joe was equal parts aloof and highly perceptive. Nevertheless, the historic imprints remained and I liked that.

Mike Marshall was the first big league ball player I met. He was injured and did not make the road trip to Baltimore and Toronto, so he came to the park just before eleven each day to do rehabilitation exercises. Marshall was a solid outfielder and first baseman who hit twenty-eight home runs with the Dodgers in 1985. Last year, he'd been a late-season acquisition from the Mets, brought in to provide a veteran bat off the bench. In a part-time role during the ALCS, he went 1-for-3 as the Sox were swept by the Oakland A's in four straight. After I met him (exact transcript: "Hi, I'm Scott." "Hi," he said.), I ran out to the concourse pay phone behind home plate to call Kate. My friends battled traffic to lifeless office parks, where they pushed papers in four-by-six cubicles; I watched baseball highlights with a man who had played in a World Series with Dodger greats Ron Cey and Steve Garvey.

Marshall didn't talk much, which was fine because I had no idea how to hold a conversation with greatness. And make no mistake about it, he was a Major League Baseball player and therefore it was magical to be near him. Marshall sat on the stationary bicycle wearing baggy mesh shorts and two days of facial growth, his sweat streaking the wall behind him and splattering on the display panel in front of him. A veteran staffer would have mocked his purple shorts or told him to shave, but during those first few days I quietly set up the machines and transferred videotapes to laserdisc, speaking only when spoken to, making sure the volume on the TV was high enough for him, and stealing glances at him when his head was down. It takes time to overcome an aura you've spent your whole life cultivating.

By late May, I'd met a handful of players, Charlie Moss the trainer, clubhouse assistants Chris and Tommy, and Tom Sneed, a Northeastern intern who worked odd jobs around the park. Joe had replaced Fitzy as the clubhouse manager (or "Clubbie") after an ugly incident in Anaheim where a man stood up along the right field seats holding a sign that read, "I was sexually assaulted by Don Fitzpatrick when I was a child." The players couldn't believe it, the coaches were disgusted, the reporters were speechless. Fitzy had worked at Fenway for decades; he knew everyone and everyone seemed to love him. When I asked Charlie if he thought it was legit, he said, "You don't stand up in front of 30,000 people holding a sign like that unless it really happened."

Years later, after victims were located and witnesses collected, Fitzpatrick would be formally charged with hiring young boys to work in the clubhouse, where he coerced them into committing horrific acts in his apartment or in the hidden nooks of Fenway. He was immediately removed from his position after the Anaheim incident, but Joe said it should've never lasted that long. Though he worked over in the visitor's clubhouse, Joe suspected something was going on, told the right people, but the owners did nothing.

A federal investigation many years later would reveal Don Fitzpatrick molested a dozen boys over a period of fourteen years. *How could that happen? Didn't anyone know?* Few secrets survive a tiny clubhouse with dozens of Sox personnel who have known each other for decades. Management knew. And it disgusted me. This wasn't like the clerical error that had resulted in the loss of catcher Carlton Fisk, or even the idiocy of trading Jeff Bagwell for Larry Andersen; ignoring heinous attacks on children extended the shortcomings of Red Sox management from incompetence to immorality. Sox management would argue they never knew, but clubhouse informants ferried all kinds of gossip upstairs: which players were out drinking late at night; who complained about playing time; who was late to batting practice. I know they knew because three people told me they told management. Their failure to respond to whatever information they had would affect management's wallet many years later to the tune of a $3 million law suit filed against Fitzpatrick and the team. Still, the whole thing made me sick, and it changed the clubhouse from this magical living museum into a filthy crime scene. For several days, I walked through the clubhouse wondering when and where this perverted monster assaulted the boys. He offered those kids a dream job, a job that should've been better than working at Disney World and going on all the rides for free, a job he would use to get to them, to trap them, confuse them. He'd ruin their childhood, their love for the Red Sox, their future.

I kept to myself, emerging from The Cave only to visit the restroom or get a soda. I was transferring key games to laserdisc and trying to learn how to chart some of the key pitchers in the league. The players knew I was in the back of the clubhouse doing something, but I was a mystery most weren't interested in solving.

Before the start of our May 30 homestand against the Orioles, I came in to work at 10:30 A.M. and saw someone stretching in the back of the weight room. Sometimes the guys from media relations or the ticket office were allowed to use the Cybex Weight machines. As long as it was early and they were out before the first player arrived, no one minded.

"I'm Mike," he said, extending his hand. He had orange hair, a chubby face, and was dressed in tight gray cotton shorts and a Montreal Canadiens sweatshirt.

I introduced myself, then flipped on the computer, laserdisc player, and monitor.

"Looks like NASA in here."

I laughed. "Not quite."

"How's it goin'?" He had a strange accent I'd never heard before.

"Pretty good. I'm still trying to figure all this stuff out."

He began rotating his torso and swirling his arms in a swimming motion.

I began watching a tape of Charles Nagy, a star pitcher from the Cleveland Indians. All the pitches looked alike. I wanted to learn to chart a game—to decipher the different pitches he threw so I could enter them into the computer program. I could tell when he threw a fastball, but he seemed to throw a dozen unique pitches; some darted inside or dropped down suddenly, others slipped away from the right-handed hitter. I couldn't consistently identify any of them. What was I supposed to do? It's not like there was a book listing what pitches he threw and how to identify them.

Nagy threw a nasty pitch that Jody Reed swung at and missed. I pounded my fist on the table.

"What the hell was that?" I said to myself.

"A slider."

I turned and looked at the man behind me.

"Oh, you're still here."

"Yep, I'm here. And it was a slider."

"You think?" I wanted to tell him to leave me alone. Go sell some tickets.

"Well, some of the players will be here soon." I returned to the computer. "I'll find out and let you know."

He laughed.

I felt bad for being abrupt.

"You worked here long?" I asked.

"My first day."

"First day?" *I was a veteran compared to this guy.* "What do you do?"

"I'm a pitcher."

Mike Gardiner had been dominating opponents for the first two months of the season. He'd been called up from Triple-A Pawtucket this morning when Dana Kiecker went on the disabled list with tendinitis in his elbow.

"So it was a slider, huh?"

"Play it again, I'll show you."

As we watched the video in super slow motion, Mike showed me the movement of the slider, which was thrown hard and had a small, late break away from a right-handed hitter.

"Nagy's got the big four: fastball, curveball, slider, change."

"How do you know?"

"You don't forget a guy with that kind of stuff. And sometimes he'll turn his fastball over and run it in on right-handed hitters."

"Turn it over?"

"He'll turn his wrist over as he delivers the fastball and it will make the ball move in a bit, kind of like a sinker. But Nagy's ball doesn't dive, it just tails in. Like mine."

"What do you throw?"

"Fastball, curve, change."

Mike looked at the clock and pulled off his sweatshirt. "Time to go. I have to get my running in."

I followed Mike out to the main clubhouse to get a soda and take a breather. A crowd of players was watching *Sports-*

Center highlights of White Sox pitcher Alex Fernandez shutting down the Mariners.

I stood behind reliever Joe Hesketh, surprised at how much thinner he looked in person than on TV. I'd only been on the inside for a few weeks and I'd already heard several players giving him a hard time. He was a notoriously slow worker, pausing for nearly twenty seconds between pitches, which irritated just about everyone in the ballpark. Incensed by Hesketh's pace, Luis Rivera said he considered charging the mound from his position at shortstop to attack his own pitcher in the fifth inning.

"Have some chocolate, skinny boy." Star left fielder, Mike Greenwell, threw a candy bar at Hesketh, hitting him in the back of the head.

Hesketh picked up the candy bar and threw it across the room, hitting backup catcher John Marzano in the rear end.

Marzano stooped to pick up the candy bar. "Who threw this at me?" Marzano said.

Hesketh kept his arms folded and his eyes on ESPN. Marzano took a step out from his locker and raised his voice. "Who pegged me in the ass with this Snickers bar? I need to know!"

Pitcher Matt Young tilted his head toward the slender culprit.

"Was it you, Hesky?"

"No, I don't know what you're talking about."

"You're a fucking liar, Hesky. A bony-ass liar." I heard a chuckle from across the room. "You know how I knew it was you who threw it?"

Hesketh stood motionless.

"Because it didn't hurt." Rivera snorted a laugh from his locker in the corner. "That weak-ass shit you throw up there couldn't knock over a house of cards."

"Watch it there, rook."

"Rook? Who the hell you calling rook?" Marzano, short and stout, had a thick Italian jaw and a smoldering fuse. He was also a renowned prankster, so players waited for clues to see if Marzie, as he was called, was really pissed off or just pretending.

"You and your seventy big league hits, that's who."

Marzano rubbed his chest with his hand and looked past Hesketh.

"Look at Hesky, would you everyone?" Marzie's booming voice shook the walls. Players turned from their lockers and waited.

"There have been thousands of games played in the history of the big leagues and hey—" Marzie noticed me standing behind Hesketh. "You, computer boy, tell me how many games have been played in the history of major league baseball."

"Thousands."

"This kid's good, fucking good." Marzie folded his hands and shifted his feet, like Billy Crystal doing a standup routine.

"So we've been playing this game for a hundred freaking years, thousands of games, and Hesky goes out there and pitches the slowest game in the history of major league baseball." Marzie put his hands on his head, exhaled. "What a slow…fucking…piece…of…shit."

"A slow *scrawny* piece of shit," added Brunansky.

"You very slow, Joe," said Tony Pena.

"Listen to this, Hesky, even Tony's gettin' on you." Marzie faced the crowd, dove into his monologue. "Hesky even drives slow. I heard he has to leave the house right after breakfast to get here for a night game. And the other night they were showing commercials in between his pitches. The friggin' network thinks he's a savior, a money-making machine. Fuck, I bet he's getting a cut of that coin. That's it!" Marzie clapped, swiveled to face Hesketh. "I knew it was inhuman to be that slow. That makes me feel better. So now it's just that Hesky is a cheap bastard selling out his teammates. Poor Luis Rivera had to have three toes amputated because he's on the balls of his feet for four hours, waiting for the damn pitcher to throw the ball. Hesky, you gonna give Luis some of that money?"

The laughter in the clubhouse reached a crescendo, until even Marzie was bent over and unable to continue.

"Marzie, cut the shit, I was only in there for one inning," said Hesketh.

For an instant, there was stillness, as if Hesketh's vulgar use of facts might force the laughter to be retracted.

"Yeah," said Brunansky, "but it lasted two hours!"

"Go to hell, all you guys!" Hesketh looked up at the TV, seeking a distraction. Joe Carter stuck out against Walt Terrell of the Tigers on a pitch low and away.

"Greenie, would you look at that slide ball!" Hesketh said.

"That be down-and-in to me, son," said Greenwell. "That shit be hammered down the line, raising chalk! Raisin' Cain! Raisin' hell!"

"Sure…"

"Yes, sir! It probably would hit some fat dude stuffing himself with ice cream." The left fielder held up two fingers. "Ground rule for two."

"Sorry, chump, but you'd never see that from me. I'd be scraping your knee with the slideball and painting the black on your foolish ass."

Greenwell kicked the batting helmet sitting on the floor beside him. "The hell you would! You slow-working sonofabitch!"

"Damn right! And you'd be out on that front foot, popping that shit up."

"Now you're bein' just silly, Hesky. Damn silly! I may have to slap some sense into your bony ass!"

"Keep away from my ass you ignorant country bumpkin." Hesketh continued, "On second thought, maybe you would get a hit out of it, though. Damn bloopy shit the other way." He stuck his rear end out, waved the bat weakly, then pranced the other way.

"Look at me, I'm Greenie bloopin' a hit!"

Jody Reed, Roger Clemens, and Carlos Quintana howled at his Greenwell imitation. Hesketh turned to face his audience. "Bloop, bloop!"

Greenwell, red-faced with anger, grasped for a final insult, but it was no use, no one was paying attention. I smiled and walked away, having no idea what the hell had just happened.

5

The Chicken Man's 4:50 Time Slot

Every morning before sunrise I'd shower, pour a bowl of Frosted Flakes, and watch the 7:00 A.M. ESPN *SportsCenter* like a stock-market whiz studying the ticker scrolling across the screen on CNN. For a few weeks, I kept a notebook on what I saw and who was playing well around the league, but upon reviewing my notes several days later, I discovered what appeared to be etchings written by a five-year-old on a crowded bus. Watching was good enough, I told myself, and I tried to make mental notes of what I saw, visualizing what players did, how their pitches moved, under what conditions base stealers took off. This was a major step forward in my development as a baseball analyst, because even with all the notes I could take and the computer data I could sort through, baseball is a visual game of swinging and throwing and running and watching an object as it flies through the air. Training the eyes to notice the subtle movements of a thrown ball and the physical habits of the participants was how you learned to analyze talent and recognize tendencies.

The coverage on ESPN was spotty, their selection of highlights aimed at pleasing the masses. If Clemens pitched, they showed him whether his performance was good, bad, or somewhere in-between. If a younger player out-pitched Clemens, it didn't matter, because people would rather watch highlights of Clemens getting bombed than some unknown kid striking out the side.

One afternoon I told pitcher Dennis Lamp I saw him on *SportsCenter.*

"The bomb I gave up to Tettleton?"

"Yup."

"Figures. Bastards won't show me punching out McLemore with the bases gassed."

He was right, of course. Good things done by average players weren't that interesting.

Most afternoons I'd sit alone in the video area with a nervous smirk on my face, looking at old tapes and counting the minutes until the first player arrived. That player was always Wade Boggs, a well-oiled hitting machine with an obscene .345 lifetime average. In 1985 he had 240 hits. He led the world in doubles. He was headed to the Hall of Fame, and I worked with him every day.

When I was in the eighth grade, I listened to Ken Coleman on the post-game show introducing this new player with the funny name. His rise to the big leagues was delayed several years because a batting champ named Carney Lansford occupied the slot at third. When Lansford was injured in a collision at the plate, Boggs had his chance and made the most of it. Lansford was traded the following year to Oakland.

On that first radio interview, Boggs was decidedly humble and well-spoken. Yes, he had hit .300 every year in the minors. No, he wasn't annoyed that the Red Sox made him spend six years tearing up the minors, waiting for a chance. Boggs described how he'd won the Triple-A batting title by .0005 of a point, beating out a young phenom for the Columbus Clippers. Coleman asked him about some of the odd routines he went through each day to prepare for a game, habits that would become legendary: eating chicken every day for lunch; taking exactly 150 grounders at exactly the same time every day; never stepping on the foul line when he walked on and off the field; drawing the Hebrew word, "Chai," in the dirt with his right cleat before each at-bat.

As a kid, I recorded every post-game interview on my black Sony boom box and listened to the tapes when the team had an off-day or a rainout. Under my bed in Winchester was a shoebox full of these old cassette tapes. If I looked hard enough I could probably find the one of Wade Boggs in 1982, a man unaware of the wild success he would have as a hitter or the imperfections that would be revealed in his character. Wade's career was magnificent, but his legacy would not be about hitting a baseball or his gold gloves or his charity work. It would be about the power of the media to exploit the tawdry details of an athlete's personal life.

In 1988, Boggs made headlines in every paper from the *New York Times* to the *National Enquirer* when it was discovered that he had a mistress whom he flew all over the country. After the story broke, he made a series of egregious mistakes, the first (and worst) was when he implicated teammates in his misadventures, violating the baseball fraternity's most sacred rule. Then, in a misguided effort to recover from the avalanche of ridicule that followed him into the hotel lobbies, the dance clubs, and the restaurants, he worked the talk show circuit. Instead of helping his cause it buried him, especially when he went on Geraldo Rivera and explained that the source of his troubles lay in the simple fact that he was "addicted to sex." What began as a repentance tour soon became a conspiracy by reporters, hosts, and talk show guests to humiliate a man who represented all that was wrong with sports heroes.

Through it all, Wade Boggs remained one of the top hitters in the game. His ability to focus on his work and enjoy continued success despite what was happening around him seemed unnatural. His life was torn apart in the papers and he hit.357. While this type of mental concentration and dedication to his craft should have been inspiring, instead it alienated Boggs—from the fans, from his friends, from his teammates. Many saw him as this freakish, sex-crazed deviant—an expressionless, lifeless, hitting robot. He was more than that. The Wade Boggs I knew was a funny, even-tempered, considerate man who was an example of hard work and dedication. He was a good friend.

But then he became a Yankee in 1993, so I can't be his friend anymore. I pretend to hate him, just like everyone else.

During our afternoon meetings in 1991, Boggs was all business, rarely engaging in small talk. He didn't ask any personal questions, and I didn't offer any information. At precisely 4:50, he would weave his way through the exercise equipment, bat in hand, and call my name, "Hey, Scotty! Let's see what you got!"

I was always ready for him.

At thirty-three years old, Wade Boggs demonstrated every evening how to hit a baseball crisply, solidly, to a location of his choosing. His beard was more red than brown, and he had thick hairy legs and a slight Southern accent that was replaced with a Midwestern accent when he was speaking to women or the press. Wade didn't speak much. Instead, he would press his lips together in what I guess could be called a smile as he passed teammates or staff in the clubhouse. Sitting next to me, slightly removed from the table, his back was gently hunched over, his elbows resting on his knees, and his folded hands on top of the knob of the bat, which stood upright, equidistant from each leg. He appeared to be using the bat as a table for his head, but he had more respect for it than that. If you asked him, he might have told you he was allowing the bat to see what had happened before. To Wade, the bat was his partner and his friend (sometimes his only friend), and in his mind they were equally responsible for his accomplishments.

Every afternoon the Sox were home, Wade and I watched video footage from the night before—a double to left, a walk, a ground ball to second. We watched every single at-bat...multiple times. He would ask me to pause the laserdisc at odd times, like just before a pitch, or as the catcher gave a signal. Sometimes he would have me replay foul balls over and over again, which was terribly irritating. What was the point in that? More than once I thought he was watching some other monitor. I rarely got to see the exciting stuff—the doubles, singles, homers—because he showed only a passing interest in reviewing the swings where he actually reached base safely. After weeks of this routine, I gathered up the nerve to ask him about it.

Minnesota was in town and we were reviewing some old at-bats against righty Jack Morris. Buried in an eight-pitch at-bat was a pitch that Boggs reached out and fouled off to the third base side (we watched it five times), another pitch low and away that he did not swing at, followed by one he fouled down the third base line. The final pitch was in the dirt for ball four. So here we were, watching the middle pitches of a walk again and again, for reasons I couldn't fathom.

The words stumbled from my mouth, "What are you looking for? Is there something you see?"

He looked over at me, stoic.

"I don't know…it seems like we're just watching these same pitches over and over and there's nothing going on. It's just a walk."

He returned to the monitor and asked to see the first pitch of the at-bat in slow motion. *I hope he's not pissed at me. Maybe I should've just kept my mouth shut.*

"Look at this," he said at last. "That's what I'm talking about. Jack's trying to go out there."

I had no idea what he was talking about.

"Jack always comes in on me. He lives in here." He motioned his hand in front of his chest.

"Late in the count he always works me in, trying to jam me. Eight years I've faced this guy and yeah, he'll show away, but the dog wants to get me out inside."

"But he walked you."

"Yeah, that's right." He took a deep breath, stroked his beard. "He had me 1-2 and goes forkball, sinker, sinker, forkball. Never comes in—just down and away." His forehead creased from the intensity of his gaze.

"Bring it back just a bit, could you?" he asked.

After the 2-2 pitch, Morris slapped his glove on his thigh and yelled something.

"I remember this right here…he was swearing at himself, pounding his glove like he missed his spot. But if you move back a bit more on the tape…" (It was a disc, but I didn't correct him.) He held his breath and his words as I shuttled the laserdisc in reverse.

"There! See?"

I did not.

"The sign!" he said.

I leaned closer to the monitor and noticed that the catcher had his index finger extended; he wiggled it toward the outside part of the plate, which meant "throw a two-seam fastball," also called a sinker.

"The bastard wanted a sinker away! Morris is so full of shit out there. He's acting like he missed his spot, so I'll think he still planned to come in on me with two strikes. But he was going for the outside corner; he never wanted to come inside. The old dog worked me, and I bought it."

"But he didn't even get you out."

"We had a guy on second, and he flings two of those weak-ass sinkers out there."

"But it's a walk, you still got on base," I offered.

"Not good enough. Next time I'll reach out there and punch that thing into left." He stood up, collected his bat and adjusted his shorts. "Those balls away are very hittable, but I'm protecting the inner half because that's what he's always done, and I'm looking to pull down the line. And when he gives me that sinker away I've got to let it go, especially if it's a borderline pitch."

"Sure, that makes sense."

"Heck, if I'm looking out over the plate or even away, I slap a single and we score a run right there. Instead, I walk and Jody grounds out to short. Inning over."

"And I thought it was just a walk."

He smiled. "Scotty, it's never *just a walk*."

Boggs stood up to go, holding the bat firmly in his left hand. "It's all about making adjustments. You know what this means, don't you?"

I shook my head. "Nope."

"Old Jack must be a little sore right now. He doesn't think he can get it in there right now." He tapped the knob of his bat, chuckled to himself. "He must be off a few miles an hour on his heater."

I had nothing valuable to add, so I returned his smile and remained silent.

"He may start using that forkball more often. Greenie's gonna like this little news flash." Boggs raised his eyebrows quickly three times in succession, like Groucho Marx.

I watched him trot through the weight room, back to the clubhouse. *I thought it was just a walk.*

My education had begun.

6

Paying Sticker Price

The radio was loud enough for me to hear Sox announcer Joe Castiglione, and quiet enough to be just another element in the surroundings. I could still hear the river, smell the fire. Kate had drifted off to sleep an hour ago, but I was wide awake. My sleep patterns were linked to the pace of the game; with each pitch my eyes counted down blinks of wakeful time. If I was tired when the game began, it didn't matter; I'd be lively by the fifth, calm by the seventh, and breathing evenly in the ninth. But extra innings were a disaster. They disrupted my sleep cycles, sending me in a direction I was powerless to predict or alter. Either I was out before the first out of the tenth, or I was shackled with restless fits of sleep until the obscene hours of the morning. I hated extra innings.

The game at Yankee Stadium went nine innings, and we beat them 6-2. The Yankees were awful, had been since the mid '80s, and I was enjoying every minute of it. And there was little cause for alarm. I'd read about this kid, Bernie Williams, coming along, but he was only one player, hardly a cure for the Yankees' lack of pitching, catching, and any decent power hitters.

In the morning, I emerged from the tent to find Kate nursing a fire.

"Sleep well?" Kate's hazel eyes were radiant, her brown hair bunched into a ponytail.

"Fine."

"We win?"

"6-2."

"Great! I love it when we beat those Yankee bastards."

I bowed my head, smothering a chuckle before it could escape. Snapping out an effective cuss word required subtle inflection and precise timing; otherwise, it had the comic ring of a Frenchman using English obscenities ("fock", "sheet"). And when Kate said this phrase, Yankees was spoken without emotion, while bastards was italicized and whispered, as if she'd just uncovered some filthy detail incriminating all Yankees past and present, and it angered her. She was disgusted. Those Yankee *Bastards.* Kate never referred to them by any other name. It was wonderful.

"Yeah, Boggs had two hits and Clemens pitched well. Sounded like a good game. I wish I could travel with the team. Wouldn't that be great?"

Kate gazed at the fire. "Who's pitching tonight?"

"Number fifty. Southpaw."

"Bolton, huh? What's he like, you've never mentioned him."

"I don't really know him. He's a quiet Southerner, hangs out with the pitchers, Young, Darwin, those guys. The other day, Greg Harris was showing him this ambidextrous glove he has."

"What is that?"

"I haven't seen it up close, but I guess it switches around to be either right-handed or left-handed."

"Why would he need that?" Kate asked.

"Harry—that's what they call him—says he can throw lefty. I've never seen him, but some of the guys say he's for real."

"That's amazing. Has anyone ever done that?"

"Pitched left-handed and right-handed? No, not that I know of. It's pretty crazy. Anyway, I don't spend much time with those guys."

"I guess you need to make a program called 'The Pitcher's Edge'."

"Yeah, once I figure out what the heck it would do!"

A loon shrieked. I looked above the tree line and followed its flight across the cloudless sky.

"Couldn't that pitcher Mike help you out?" Kate asked.

"Probably. Gardy's mentioned these paper charts they use for the pitchers, but I don't know much about them. Half the team are pitchers, so I guess I'd better figure out how to help them if I want to stick around."

Kate prodded the fire with a stick, then set it down on the ground beside her. "I was gonna boil some water for oatmeal. Want some?"

"Sure," I said. "Did you remember to pack the Folgers coffee packets, those ones that are like tea bags?"

"Me? You said you were going to pack all the food."

"Oh."

Kate pulled out a red and black box from the cooler. "But I knew you'd forget, so I did it right before we left."

I stuck out my tongue, then got the bowls and mugs from the backpack in the tent.

"Lou's never even checked in on me once, you realize that?" She had her head down, fiddling with the jackknife. "Wouldn't you think he'd come down to see how it's going?"

"Maybe Joe Morgan's telling him."

"Morgan!" I said, louder than I expected. "Right! He doesn't even know my name, has no idea what I'm doing back there!"

"Hey, settle down tough guy, you'll wake our fellow campers."

I looked through the trees at a blue tent thirty yards away. "Sorry!" I whispered. "Anyway, I don't think Morgan will survive unless we win the division."

"Really?"

"Jack Clark can't stand him, and a few of the other guys just think he's senile. Some of the moves he makes are just foolish, like taking out Harris and bringing in Fossas the other night."

The water boiled over, hissing on the rocks surrounding our fire.

"Should you ask some of the players to tell Lou, or even Morgan, what a good job you're doing?"

"I couldn't. It would be too awkward. Besides, I don't even know if I'm doing a good job."

"C'mon! What about what Reardon said to you that time? And Boggs comes and visits you every day. That sounds like success to me."

"I wish you were the GM," I said.

"I could do that job."

"You'd have to call the Yankees occasionally to discuss possible trades."

"Forget it, I don't want the job."

Kate watched as I used two sticks to guide the boiling water pot off the steel grate and onto the picnic table.

"Now, how come at home you'll spill a glass of milk every other night, but out here you can remove a warped pot of water from a raging fire with two twigs and not spill a drop?"

"I love the challenge, I guess!"

I tossed the sticks into the fire, poured us each two packets of oatmeal (did anyone ever eat just one?), and settled into my fireside camping chair.

"So let me tell you about Ellis. I've been waiting for weeks. You work too much."

"Me? You just worked ten days in a row, twelve hours a day!"

I shrugged. "Anyway, I've been working with Ellis a lot. He's a great guy."

"I was worried it would be a disappointment when you met him."

Ellis Burks had been my favorite player since he'd come up in 1987. He was smooth in the outfield, had great speed, and hit for power and average. Ellis played hard, didn't show up the opposing pitcher when he went deep, and rarely spoke with reporters.

"He's only a few years older than me."

"What is he, twenty-seven?"

"Twenty-six."

"He seems like he's all business."

"No, not at all. He's always cuttin' on other guys. Hesketh, Jody, Greenwell. In a nice way though, not swearing or putting people down like Greenwell does. He's just looking to make jokes, have fun."

"Where's he from?"

"Texas."

I poured the hot water into Kate's bowl, then did the same to mine.

"You know how he talks with that Southern accent?"

"I can't really remember…"

"Well, he does. And he'll always use words incorrectly to sound like a hick. It's strange, most guys want to sound smarter, Ellis wants to sound dumber."

"Maybe it's to protect himself."

"He was telling me this story about how he got his new Mercedes."

"Tough life…"

"Well, let me start by saying that most guys will do favors to get free stuff or good deals."

"Like what?" asked Kate.

"Sign autographs. Coach a kid's baseball team for a day."

"And what do they get?"

"Heck, I know Pena gets free suits, shoes, stuff like that. And Jody got a great deal on that new truck he bought."

"But they're making millions! They don't need special deals!"

"I know, but that's not the point. Anyway, Ellis doesn't do that. So last winter he's at home in Texas working on his truck when he suddenly decides to check out the new Mercedes Boggs was raving about last season."

"It must be nice. We should get one…"

"Yeah, so he jumps in his truck and heads to the Fort Worth dealership. The sales guys give him dirty looks, then finally someone comes up to him and asks him to leave. Never asks him if he's thinking of purchasing a car or if he'd like a test drive. They just see this guy…I don't know…anyway, they just told him to leave.

"Ellis said to the guy, 'I want to look at one of these cars.'"

"Well, you've looked long enough, so why don't you just be on your way there, fella?"

"Ellis drove to the nearest dealership, which was an hour away, and bought a new Mercedes. That evening, he returned to the first dealership in his silver Mercedes, pulled it right up in front, and walked up to the salesman who'd dismissed him hours earlier.

"It's a beauty, isn't it," Ellis said. "What do you think?"

"Hey, you were that—" the salesman stammered.

"That scumbag you threw out on the street? Yeah, that's me." Ellis rubbed the fender of his new car.

"But sir, I'm really–"

"Really what?"

The salesman stood hard and still, like a mannequin.

"And it would've been a heck of a sale." Ellis ambled to the front of the car and caressed the silver hood ornament with his index finger. "I paid sticker, 'cause I'm not in to all that haggl-in' and shit."

Ellis cackled and revealed a devious grin.

"You don't know who I am, and that's good. I'm no one special, just a ballplayer who wanted to buy a car." Ellis back-pedaled toward the car door and gently lifted the handle. "Next time you turn someone away, think of me. Think of all the cash you lost. And get that shit straightened out."

Kate was smiling ear to ear.

7

A Fly on the Wall

Twenty-five players, two trainers, six coaches, five clubhouse guys, and one video guy spent most of their workday in a bustling area roughly the size of a basketball court. On weekends, family members were allowed in the clubhouse the morning before the game. The Reebok and Nike sneaker reps distributed free samples of batting gloves, shirts, and spikes. Jody Reed and his agent discussed contract incentives in front of his locker. Singer Bruce Hornsby visited. Stephen King chatted with the players one Saturday after a game. (Marzano: "Can you write a book about a catcher who runs around with all his gear on, killing people?" King: "I'll work on it.") Cellular phones were becoming available (Jeff Reardon's friend at CellularOne sold them for $350), so players regularly spoke to buddies, family members, and "lady" friends within earshot of teammates. There was no privacy. I did my best to be seen but not stand out, to hear things but not be labeled an eavesdropper, to chat with people but not be an annoyance.

Long before my time, an unspoken clubhouse hierarchy was constructed based on a blend of talent, personality, and time-served. To better understand this subculture, I created

labels based on what I'd observed and been told. The food
chain, from top-to-bottom, consisted of star veterans, drifters,
upstarts, guys-on-the bubble, staff, and rookies. Star veterans
had all the perks: first in line at post-game spread, choice of
batting practice slot, the second bus on the road (which had
no reporters, coaches or staff). Getting to the top of the ladder
was more than just time-served. You could have six years in,
but if you bounced around from team to team without ever
putting up numbers you'd be a drifter, like Joe Hesketh or
Dennis Lamp.

Despite similarities in time-served, the top two groups, star
veterans and drifters, received very different treatment from
fans, other players, and the media. When Jack Clark was
signed over the winter it was front-page news. The *Globe* ran
an upbeat feature story, a meaty article analyzing his career
stats and projecting his Fenway numbers, and a color picture
of a smiling Jack in his new number twenty-five Red Sox jersey. When drifter Dennis Lamp was acquired, it was buried in
the sports transaction log, right below the blurb announcing
the new women's volleyball coach for Pepperdine University.

Naehring, Bolton, Dopson, Reed, and Quintana were
established younger guys, upstarts who had a few years in the
big leagues and had earned the respect of the veterans. They
were below the drifters based on time served, but were more
popular with fans, and got more attention from the media.
Lowest on the food chain were the rookies, unproven young
players with less than a year in the big leagues. They were
expected to be quiet and respectful, take any and all shit other
players handed out, bring out the bag of goodies (gum, chew,

sunflower seeds) to the bullpen, do the ball bucket during extra batting practice, and sit on the first bus on road trips.

Some players escaped classification: Ellis had only four years in, but he put up numbers, was respectful of the older guys, and played the game hard, so he could hang with star veterans Clark, Greenwell, Clemens, Pena, Boggs, Darwin, and Brunansky. A classic drifter was Greg Harris, who at thirty-five had ten years in, put up some solid numbers, but bounced to six teams in nine years and was somewhat of an oddball. He could say what he wanted, do what he wanted, but he wasn't a star veteran, never would be. Kevin Romine had four years in as a part-time player, but could be gone tomorrow. A guy-on-the-bubble. Drifters generally outranked upstarts on the food chain, but exceptions were made based on personality and talent. Naehring, an upstart, had higher clubhouse stature than Hesketh, a drifter. The caste system was flexible.

Interaction between members of hierarchical groups was based on their participation in activities groups, a few of which were the Bible-bangers (born-again Christians who held chapel in the showers on Sundays), poker-players, golfers, and outdoorsmen. Ellis was a member of the poker-players activities group, which was heavily veteran-based. Rookies were not allowed into this group, and drifters such as Hesketh were admitted on a case-by-case basis, depending on whether the veterans thought they could take his money or not.

Cultural subgroups often formed activities subgroups. A lot of the Latinos (Fossas, Rivera, Pena) were Bible-bangers. The veterans were typically poker players. Rookies and guys-on-the-bubble didn't have as much money as the other guys, so they didn't golf and weren't allowed to play poker with the veterans. And then there was the NASCAR group, the hunting group, and the country-music group, all with the exact same members (a.k.a. the Greenwell Group). My system was limited and simplistic, but it helped me order this world and find my way around in it.

If I traveled with the team, I'd have been in the staff group, consisting of the trainers, clubhouse guys and coaches. The coaches mixed well with the star veterans because they were close in age and most coaches were former players. Staff members seemed to associate with rookies and bubble-guys because they had similar income levels, were around the same age, and could dine out on the road without being recognized and creating a fuss.

While in the main area of the clubhouse, I locker-hopped to keep from lingering at a venue, or inappropriately participating in a conversation approved for my ears but not my mouth. If I made the players alter their conversation in any way because I was present, then I'd be seen in the same light as the front-office buffoons, or worse still, as a reporter. I was respectful but not fawning, aloof but not cocky. I measured every word and action, bottled my reactions to obscene comments and shocking events, and feigned disinterest unless being spoken to directly.

When I heard Jack Clark say to Brunansky, "My accountant says I've got no money," I kept talking to Mike Gardiner, didn't whisper anything to him, didn't turn my head.

"Well, stop buying so many damn cars, Jack!" said Brunansky. The following year Clark filed for bankruptcy, having disposed of several multi-million dollar salaries. At the time of filing, Clark owned eighteen automobiles.

When I heard a married player arranging dinner with his girlfriend on his cell phone, or players comparing notes on illegal drug supplements, steroids, or drinking binges, I filed the details, but never spoke of it to anyone.

When I carried a cup of coffee over to Joe, who was doing paperwork at the gray table, and heard Clemens arranging a clandestine meeting with a sick kid at Children's Hospital, I kept this knowledge to myself.

I learned the ropes by studying Clubhouse Manager Joe Cochran, whose job it was to get along with everyone. To the best of my knowledge, these were the top three unwritten rules:

1. No chatter.

Meaningless dialog was acceptable at other jobs, but not here. The mainstays "How 'bout this weather?" and "How was the weekend?" were off-limits. As was this classic exchange of nothingness:

"What's up?"

"Not much, how 'bout you?"

"Oh, not too much."

And its ugly cousin:

"How's it goin'?"

"Not too bad, how 'bout you?"

"Pretty good."

Eleven useless words, ice-breakers for office acquaintances and the socially inept. Here, close confines bred familiarity and the chatterboxes were reformed or weeded out in Double-A. Players saw each other all day, every day—including weekends and holidays—and this needless banter wore them down.

2. Don't be a green fly.

I believe the term originated from a certain type of insect that hovers over rotting animal carcasses, feeding off the remains. Translation: Don't badger players for autographs. Don't ask them to step outside and meet your friends. Don't be a green fly.

3. No big-leaguing.

As Joe explained it to me, if you're talking to Tom Bolton and Clemens calls your name, finish the conversation with Bolton. Don't cut him off and rush over to the high-salaried superstar, leaving the "little guy" hanging. While the veterans deserved respect, it should not be at the expense of the other players or staff. Big-leaguing was considered a heinous offense.

Life in the clubhouse was accelerated. The games came and went each day, so players didn't waste time feeling each other out. They became quick friends or fierce enemies. During the day in the clubhouse and at night on the field, players found out who they could trust and who they couldn't, who they liked and who they disdained, who was out for himself and who was a team guy. It was a rush to judgment, sometimes on a first impression or the words of another player, but mostly founded on refined character-recognition skills developed through high school, college, or the minor leagues. All the players in the clubhouse had been stars on their little league teams, heroes in high school, can't-miss-kids in college. They received special treatment most of their lives. They met people from all walks of life. They'd been watched with adoring eyes, shuffled to the front of the line at dance clubs, given free clothes. Strangers ordered them beers and showered them with trite words wishing them luck.

Brunansky could tell by the way someone approached him if they were going to ask him for something. Greenwell studied a victim's reaction to his verbal abuse, which he considered an effective way to judge character. Would they lash back or take it in stride? Tim Naehring could talk to you for five minutes, make you believe you're special and he's your best friend, then not remember the conversation an hour later. Aside from hitting and throwing a baseball for a few hours a day, these men dealt with people—their friends, other players, reporters, women, countless fans. They were professionals at interacting with and understanding people, always on their terms.

The coffee machine was our office water cooler, and it heard outrageous tales of escapades with women, drinking until the early-morning hours, golfing exploits, and poker winnings. The first time I poured a cup of the clubhouse brew and raised it to my lips, I gagged and inspected the contents, uncertain whether I should toss it in the trash or pour several pots into a five-gallon bucket, take it home, and slap it on my driveway. Chris, the red-headed twenty-year-old batboy, made the coffee but did not drink it. A bad sign. One morning I caught him with a cup of Dunkin' Donuts coffee a few hours before the players arrived.

"Chris, why don't you make some of that fine European blend you prepare for us every day?"

"You crazy? European? It's from some guy in Lawrence. Calls his company 'Best Coffee.' The stuff is brutal."

It was bad, but culpability for the shortcomings of the coffee extended beyond the quality of the product; preparation was a contributing factor. I'd watched Chris measure the coffee grounds and place them in the filter with all the precision of a gravedigger flinging shovelfuls of earth over his shoulder. Nevertheless, everyone drank this ghastly sludge even when it was ninety degrees and humid. Chris blew through six pots on an average day. I often loitered by the coffee machine and eavesdropped, not because the tales were exceedingly interesting (after the first few they all sounded the same), but so I could be visible, talk with guys, and gain trust, which might result in more usage of my system. And after several weeks of adjustment (and the benefit of three sugars and four creams), I was able to hold down nearly a full six-ounce cup of coffee.

As I lingered and listened, the words I heard made my ears blush. Profanity was the glue that held most phrases together, and it took some getting used to. Obscenities and swearwords were used as adjectives, adverbs, nouns, and verbs. They were hyphenated to create multi-syllabic, more explosive expletives. Parts of the human anatomy and various species of pond life could serve as bookends to a curse word, making it more colorful. These ghastly creations were thrown into causal conversations by players as if they were staples of the English language. Sometimes they'd be adopted by another player and a new word was born. From here they'd spread to different teams, and league-wide adoption could take place. You could say whatever you wanted; there was no co-worker in the wings rushing off to squeal, because there was no one to squeal to—there was no human resources department. I soon adopted the lexicon of my workplace and used many of these same words. It became a habit that drew criticism when I accidentally carried words home to Kate, hilarity when I wielded them in conversations with my friends.

My workday consisted of a number of quick visits from just a handful of people. I spent a lot of time alone watching old tapes of Erickson, Morris, Stewart, Mussina, and McDowell. There were no meetings, no status reports, no manager evaluating my progress. My father thought I'd been "thrown to the wolves," that I was an outsider with some fancy machines trying to integrate a system with a bunch of techno-phobic ball players. When he learned of the lack of guidance I'd been given from Lou and manager Joe Morgan's disdain for technology, he told me there was no way this could be a success.

"You need an advocate. You need someone to help you learn what the players need, someone who can help sell it," he said.

Boggs didn't offer to promote my services to the team and I wasn't entirely disappointed; he was a fabulous hitter and he believed in the system, but his battles with Clemens had left him on the other side of the tracks. Aligning with Boggs would have cut me off from Clemens, Brunansky, Pena and Greenwell. I needed someone more popular, who was well-respected, and who had not taken sides in the Clemens-Boggs conflict.

The turning point came in June, when twenty-four-year-old shortstop Tim Naehring went on the sixty-day disabled list with a back injury that would badger him throughout his major league career. He won the starting job from Rivera in spring training and got off to a decent start in April, but his back pain became too much. He tried to play through it, but was rewarded with an 0-for-36 at the plate and a trip to the disabled list. Each day he came in early for medical treatment and received a stack of fan mail from Joe, a rubdown from therapist Rich Zawacki and the run-around from Dr. Pappas. Just after the national anthem, he began his workout in the weight room, adjacent to my place of business.

Tim had a Matt Damon smile and thick brown hair that remained perfectly styled even after nine innings of compression under a sweaty baseball cap. Naehring was the new breed of shortstop, in the mold of Cal Ripken: over six-feet tall and wide-shouldered, with quick footwork around the bag, terrific range up the middle, quick wrists at the plate, and a sure-handed glove in the field. Twenty-five to thirty homer potential. Before Jeter and A-Rod, before Nomar and Tejada, there was only Ripken. And Naehring was the next Ripken. His career lay ahead of him, and he approached it with the puckered-mouth poise of someone unfamiliar with failure.

Tim rode the exercise bike, facing the video area, for forty-five minutes each day at the end of his workout.

"What are you doin' there, buddy?"

"Isolating a feed from Camera Two and capturing it on S-VHS."

He closed his eyes, shook his head. "Huh?"

"Okay, sorry." I took a deep breath. "There's a camera in center that's always focused on home plate. I'm recording the feed from that camera to a tape so I can see the catcher's sign and learn what pitches are being thrown."

"You got one from yesterday? Pop it in one of these other machines, and we'll take a look."

I reached for the tape. "Great, 'cause I have no friggin' idea how to tell a slider from a forkball."

"A slider will move away from a right-hander, a forkball will usually move straight down." He simulated the path of the ball with his hand. "It's called, 'falling off the table.' It comes in straight and hard, then dives down at the last second."

We watched a Jack McDowell pitch come in straight, then suddenly drop down, across the hitter's ankles.

"Forkball. McDowell's best pitch. It gets me every time."

"Why don't you just lay off it? Don't swing."

He laughed. "It looks like a fastball right over the heart of the plate. You can't help but take a hack. But then it's gone."

"Look at this." I paused the tape, rewound it, and played it frame by frame. "Jody didn't swing at the forkball."

"Yeah, you're right. Play the whole at-bat."

Jody Reed fouled off the next pitch.

"I remember this one. Jody was guessing, waiting for the curveball."

Tim elbowed me in the shoulder. "Watch what happens when you look curveball," he said. The next pitch was a fastball right down the middle, a called third strike.

"Veteran move right there. Jody didn't swing at the forkball with one strike, so Jack knows he's guessing, waiting for something off-speed. So he doesn't give it to him. He gets him to foul off a pitch away, then grooves him a heater, knowing he's not ready for it. And Jody sits there with the bat on his shoulder."

"Damn."

I watched the pitch sequence again.

"Tim, how did you learn all this stuff? It's like you've been in the league for ten years."

"Just seeing a lot of pitches, paying attention. Talking to veterans, writing stuff down. Ask questions, Scotty, guys will help you."

Naehring's advice and support gave me hope that computers and video equipment, mixed with scouting expertise, might one day change major league baseball.

8

A Legend Arrives

"It's like a carnival out there," said Jody Reed.

It was a steamy afternoon in July, just before batting practice, and a few players sought refuge from the heat in the air conditioning of The Cave. Jody was using the remote-control camera to zoom in on the donut of reporters surrounding the newest arrival from Pawtucket.

Brunansky clicked his tongue in disgust.

"A lot of guys rake in Triple-A. Let's see what he does when Randy Johnson shows him that inside gas."

Naehring chimed in, "I don't know how he'll do against The Big Unit, but my boy Mo can hit a little bit."

In big league parlance, "a little bit" meant he was an exceptional player. Not all descriptions were understated, however, as a catcher with a strong arm was said to have a "hose." To "rake" was to hit very well for an extended period of time. Pitchers who had fastballs in the mid-nineties threw "cheese."

"He's a big-ass dude, that's for damn sure," said Brunansky.

"What number is he wearing?" asked Reed.

Naehring rose from the weight bench. "Forty-two."

"They'll make a big deal about that."

"Why?" asked pitcher John Dopson.

"Dammit, Dopper, please tell me you're kidding!"

"Sorry, I ain't kiddin'," he said.

"Have you no respect for this game?" asked Jody.

"Not really. I just throw my two-seamer and try to make enough coin so I can keep my fishin' boat."

"Hell, Dopper, forty-two was Jackie Robinson's number."

Dopson stared blankly ahead, waiting for the rest of the story.

"He was the first black player in the big leagues," said Brunansky.

"Oh, yeah, I hearda him. Dodgers, right?"

"Yeah, Mo gettin' his number was a smooth move." Naehring paused and smiled. "Mo's gonna make it big here. Heck, he's already a damn legend."

Mo Vaughn was a legend, despite having exactly zero big league at-bats under his belt. I'd heard about the gargantuan homers he'd clobbered in the minors, I'd seen pictures of his massive biceps in a Pawtucket baseball magazine, and I'd watched his cocky home run trot when they showed minor league highlights on NESN. Now Mo Vaughn was here, in Boston, and it was a big deal.

Mike Gardiner entered The Cave and sat down next to Brunansky. "Would you look at our boy Mo!" he said.

"Damn rookies." Brunansky got up from his chair, looked down at Gardy, and hissed, "They're such a nuisance."

Brunansky departed, and Reed followed behind him.

"Hey, Gardy," I said.

"Hey, Mr. Video!"

"Mr. Video, huh?" asked Tim. "Is that what everyone calls you now, Scotty?"

"This is the first I've heard of it."

"Not bad, huh?" Gardy twisted his neck back to look at Naehring.

"Naw, something's missing. He needs something more dynamic. Heck, he's got the USS Enterprise back here with all these screens and buttons and computers."

"You watch *Star Trek*, don't you, Scotty?" asked Naehring.

"No. Never."

"Yeah, you do. C'mon, I know you love it! All techie guys watch that."

Ellis came back, holding a large cup of ice water, and sat silently watching the commotion behind home plate.

"I don't watch it!"

Gardy chuckled and nodded back at Naehring. "Gettin' a little worked up here, isn't he?"

"Ha!" said Tim. "I think he's all into that *Star Trek* gig. Probably got a huge poster of the Enterprise in the family room of his apartment. His girl Kate begs him to take that shit down, but he won't budge. It's the first thing you see when you walk in his front door."

I was staring at the TV trying not to laugh. Tim came closer, leaned in just inches from my ear, and said, "To boldly go where no man has gone before!"

"I hate that damn show!" I said.

"What do you think, Ellis?"

"'Bout what?"

"Scotty here and Star Trek. Gardy and I think he loves that show, probably sits back here with all this video equipment and pretends he's Captain Kirk."

Ellis smiled. "Like he's Captain Video or some shit."

"That's it! Captain Video!" exclaimed Tim.

"That's perfect," said Gardy. "Captain Video."

Nicknames are assigned to you, unless you're a superstar athlete or a rock star or an actor. I wasn't any of these things, so mine was slapped on me, without my consent.

As I grabbed a soda after the game (we beat Jamie Navarro and the Brewers 6-0), Tim yelled out at the top of his lungs, "Captain Video, report to the bridge! The Enterprise is encountering hostile spacecraft!"

"Hey, Captain!" Brunansky said. "Can't you press some damn buttons back there and make Finley's slider straighten out?"

"Sorry, Bruno, can't do that."

"Then what the hell good are you?"

The next day, when I walked through the trainer's room, Charlie looked up from his laptop, "Well, if it isn't Captain *Fucking* Video."

"Charlie, can I ask you something?"

"Fuck no."

"Is there any way of gettin' rid of that nickname?"

"Fuck no."

"Really?"

"Really."

"O.K. Thanks, Charlie."

And though I didn't embrace the name while I was at work, I detailed its origination and usage to my friends, my father, and Kate. It was a sign of acceptance, of some limited team-wide acknowledgement of my role inside these exclusive walls. Captain Video wouldn't have been my first choice of nicknames, but it could have been worse. At least now everyone knew who I was. The assignment of this name was on the outskirts of affection, an athlete's way of saying "you're O.K., we think we'll keep you for a while." Ellis, Tim, and Gardy's selection was careful—more light-hearted than condescending—and an undeniable first step toward acceptance. Those who used it would be stepping over to my side, casting a vote in an election in which I was running unopposed, but still could lose.

I often ventured into the main clubhouse area, blending into the surroundings, but half wanting to be noticed, to be called by name (or nickname), which might ultimately lead to wider use of the system. In my mini-marketing plan, the nickname was a tagline I could use to improve sales. Brand recognition was up, as evidenced by several interactions that took place in early August.

Chris, the bat boy, was emptying the trash barrel in the clubhouse and looked over and saw me talking to Joe. He saluted me and sang in an opera-like voice, "Helloooo, Captain Videoooo."

Clemens nodded and smiled, "Awright, looks like we got our boy a new name!"

Ellis said to Greenwell, "That ball in the gap last night hit a damn sprinkler head."

"It looked funky, but I don't think so, Ellis. It was probably just a divot or something."

"C'mon now, Greenie, I saw it myself back there with Cap'n Video. He'll put it up on the big screen back there and show you."

Greenwell nodded, "O.K., I may have to go check that shit out. Damn sprinkler heads, can't they hide 'em any better than that?"

The more I urged people to call me by my real name, the more they called me Captain Video. Even when it was neither necessary nor appropriate to address me, players would call out my nickname.

Carlos Quintana was a bulky man with a crooked smile, a wry sense of humor, and a sweet inside-out swing. He didn't speak unless he had something funny to say. Joe thought he must've learned English watching David Letterman. I'd never worked with Carlos, but I'd introduced myself and said hello a few times in passing. I could feel his eyes on me as I walked through the clubhouse. Carlos's voice bellowed like a Latin-American Darth Vader, "Cawp-ton Veee-dee-oooo."

Then he repeated it, louder, slower: "Cawp-ton Veee-dee-oooo." It took several seconds for him to finish.

The first few times he did this, I stopped and waited to see if he actually wanted to speak to me, but after the third time I just smiled and waved, as players cackled and begged him to say it again. This was on the edge of mockery, and Ms. Sheridan, my second grade teacher, may have classified it as "laughing at" rather than "laughing with," but the lines were blurry enough for me to see it as "with" and continue about my business.

Four days before Mo Vaughn's arrival, we were in first place, coming off a sensational sweep of the Athletics at Fenway in which Gray, Bolton and Harris each earned a win. Roughly a month later we found ourselves in fourth place, nine games out of first. Yes, it was a long season and you're supposed to keep an even keel and all that, but when no one's getting hits, the pitchers are getting lit up, and the team is inventing new ways to lose, all that "one day at a time" bullshit goes out the window and players snap.

The low point of the past month came on a Sunday afternoon against Minnesota. Last year's Twins finished at the bottom of the AL West, but this was a different squad. Veterans Kirby Puckett, Dave Winfield, and Kent Hrbek were energized by rookie second baseman Chuck Knoblauch and pitcher Scott Erickson. The addition of Jack Morris brought stability to the pitching staff. The Twins used the Red Sox as a tackling dummy in their climb to the top of the American League Central.

The Twins took the first three games of the series, and were pounding us 14-1 in the fourth game when Joe Morgan decided to let utility player Steve Lyons pitch. It gave the fans something to cheer about and the writers something to write about, but it made a mockery of our pitching staff and embarrassed the team. Maybe that's what Morgan wanted. Lyons surrendered two hits in one inning of relief, but the Twins didn't score off him, which was more than you could say about most of our real pitchers.

There will never be another Steve Lyons. He was a hustling player with marginal talent who was erratic in the field and on the basepaths, earning him the nickname "Psycho." In 1990, I saw him execute the "hidden ball trick"to perfection. Following a head-first slide, he once mistakenly pulled down his pants while shaking dirt out of his belt. Lyons was handsome and articulate and the camera loved him, which made some players jealous, others mildly annoyed. When asked to cite Lyons' greatest asset as a player, frustrated Chicago White Sox manager Jeff Torborg replied, "Interviews."

When he was reacquired from Chicago in 1991, one of the clubbies handed out T-shirts with "Psycho II" on the front to celebrate the return of this entertaining player. It was an amusing nickname, but it didn't fit. Sure he was fiery, but he wasn't violent or angry like a psycho; he was erratic and aggressive and acted like an airhead sometimes. "Dizzy" would have been a better choice. Or "freak show."

To his credit, Lyons knew how to get the most out of his ability. His swing wasn't one you'd use to instruct the little leaguers—crouched over, poor weight transfer, reaching too much—but he got hits when he had to, moved runners along, bunted well and stayed in the lineup because he could play so many positions. In 1991, he played first, second, third, left, center, right and pitcher for the Red Sox. Though he had the skills to play short and catcher, Morgan wasn't ready to turn the season into a circus. In a spring training game, while with the White Sox, Lyons played every position in a single game. He was a Freak Show.

As the Minnesota blowout came to a close, Greenwell celebrated his 0-for-3 with a visit to my place of business. He paced back and forth in the back of the weight room, bat in hand, mumbling to himself.

John Dopson was standing behind me doing his rehab exercises. "Uh-oh," he said.

Sean McDonough's play-by-play was interrupted by the earsplitting ring of bat on steel. Dopson and I held our breath and kept still, like hunters waiting for a bear to pass. When the banging stopped, we exhaled. After we heard the click of his metal spikes on the tile of the trainer's room, we rushed back to inspect the damage. Pieces of chipped-off bat covered the carpet, the plastic seat cushion of the Cybex machine was torn to shreds, and the metal rods that guided the plates up and down were bent.

"Greenie is one crazy fella."

"At least he cares," I said.

"He's like a little kid having a tantrum."

"Yeah, go tell him that."

Dopson was taller and wider than Greenwell, but was passive and soft in the middle. "He'd kill me!"

"Yeah, he would."

"You wouldn't even recognize me after he was through with me."

"You're right. We'd need to use your dental records. Try to keep them handy, would you? I'm going to pass on your remarks to Mr. Greenwell."

"Don't even joke about that, Scotty. I'd be a dead man!"

9

Fixing the Splitter

I peered through the bars of the lat pull-down machine and saw Jeff Gray waiting for me, his white, number thirty-eight game jersey glowing from across the room.

"Has Gray been there long?" I whispered to Charlie.

"Ten minutes. The guy's a nut," Charlie countered my whisper with a booming jab. "It's seven hours before first pitch, for Christ's sake, and he's got his game-whites on."

"Charlie, you talking about me?" Gray said from across the room.

"You're a nut, Jeff. I told you that to your face last week."

"I love you too, Charlie."

"Who said anything about love? I don't love you. You're just a goddamned ballplayer, a middle-reliever."

I stepped over the dumbbells, but caught a toe on one of the forty-five pound plates scattered on the floor by the weight bench, banging my knee on the side of the triceps extension machine.

Charlie continued, "Shit, you don't know what love is. Love ain't some fat, old trainer. You're a scary bastard Gray, saying all this about love. Love ain't shit, that's what I told my first wife when she took everything I had."

I continued walking and cursed through clenched teeth as I rubbed my knee.

Gray turned around suddenly. "You O.K.?"

"Fine. It happens a few times a week."

I sat beside Gray and turned on the 32-inch TV monitor. "Jeff, you've been dealin' lately!"

Gray had an ERA near two and his hits-to-innings-pitched ratio was microscopic. He was our set-up guy, the pitcher who came into the game in the seventh or eighth and held the lead until the closer could finish it off.

"Thanks, Scotty, but the last few games I haven't felt right out there. The splitter's been flat."

"Rich, Joe!" yelled Charlie. "Jeff Gray, the set-up guy, number thirty-eight, is back here talking about love. C'mon in. We'd rather be at the beach, or golfing, and he's happy to be here half a day before first pitch, in his game jersey, tellin' me and Scotty about love."

"So Jeff, what can I help you with?" I asked.

"Well, I was wondering if I could see my outing from last night." As he spoke, he opened his mouth a bit more than was required, giving singular attention to each word before moving to the next.

"Sure." I fumbled for the laserdisc that contained his last appearance against Chicago. "Hey, sorry I'm late."

"No, you're not late, I'm early. You've got things you need to do, I don't expect you to spend every minute here."

"It just looked like you were waiting for me."

"No, I was just relaxing back here. It's quiet. Comfortable."

"A lot of players say that."

"Yeah, sometimes all this stuff goes by so fast. It's good to just sit back here and remember what we're all doing."

"What we're doing?"

"We're here." He looked back over his shoulder at the weight machines, at Charlie Moss working on his computer. "We're part of the Red Sox!"

As a journeyman who'd bounced around in Triple-A for five years, Gray still had the dust of minor league life on his lips. He was in the big leagues now, and he enjoyed tasting the difference.

"It's air-conditioned here," Gray said. He looked at me, expecting a reaction. "And there are candy bars and soda pop out by my locker. If I want a candy bar I just take one. How about that?"

I laughed and returned his smile. "Yeah, that's a sweet deal, isn't it?"

"Pay Day. That's my favorite. It's the one in the white wrapper, with all the nuts. You know it?"

"Yeah, but I've never had one."

"Heck, I could down those all day long!" he said. He clapped his hands, then rubbed them together. "O.K., let's look at some video. I've got to see where I'm releasing the splitter. Fish says it's slipping out a bit early."

"What the hell does that old man know?"

It was Jeff Reardon, an ice pack fastened to his shoulder with ace bandages, making his way to where we were sitting.

"I can say that," Reardon said, "because I'm an old man myself."

"Didn't you and Fish go to school together?" It was Charlie again, a part of every conversation despite being fifty feet away.

"Not quite, Charlie," said Reardon.

Bill Fischer was the sixty-two-year-old pitching coach, the man responsible for Clemens' remarkable development; he was a quiet man with a red nose that was wrinkled like a raisin.

"Can you give those guys some love, Term?" yelled Charlie from his desk. "That's what they're after. It's like the god-damned '60s back there in the video area."

He sat down behind me, never looking back at Charlie.

"Yeah, I'm old," Reardon mused. "Every single muscle hurts after I pitch. I can remember when I'd wake up and not be able to tell if I'd pitched the day before. Gettin' old sucks."

"I can only hope I last as long as you have, Term," Gray said.

Jeff Reardon was one of the best relievers in the game; a black-bearded closer who came in and threw either his blistering heater or his nasty curve to record three outs in the ninth. Most players called him Term, short for "The Terminator." It started as a family joke; his brother-in-law had a shirt printed with a burly caricature of Reardon blowing a ball by a cowardly hitter. In thick black letters along the bottom were the words, "The Terminator." Reardon wore the shirt once under his uniform and struck out the side; now he wore it every game for good luck. Soon several dozen of these shirts found their way into the clubhouse and were worn proudly by players, the clubhouse guys, and the ground crew. Joe gave me one of these shirts, and I still have it.

"What are we watching?"

"Scotty here is showing me what's wrong with my splitter."

"He is, is he?" Reardon slapped my shoulder. "You know a lot about pitching, do you?"

"No, not really. I'm just showing him the video."

"All right, let's see what's going on with this."

We directed our attention to the large monitor, where White Sox catcher Ron Karkovice hit a 2-1 pitch off the wall for a double.

"O.K., bring it back, would you?" asked Reardon.

I reversed the laserdisc, and we watched it again. On the third pitch Reardon leaned in, tapped my shoulder and said, "Hold it! That's the one. That's the pitch you need to look at, Jeff."

"What do you see, Term?"

"One more time, Scotty, bring us back." *If I had a dollar for every time I heard that during my tenure with the Red Sox, I could've earned close to Clemens' $3 million salary.*

Gray stared silently at the screen, awaiting input from the elder statesman of the Red Sox bullpen.

"Your release points are different. On that nasty first-pitch splitter you're right here." Reardon stood up, put his right arm out beside him in an "L."

"But on the 1-1 pitch your release point is in tighter." He moved his hand two inches closer to his head. "You're not up top, your release is drifting in and it takes away from the bite on the splitter."

Gray stood up to face Reardon, picked up a ball from the table, and did a mock windup, freezing as he came to the release point.

"See, you're doing it now! Same thing!" Reardon leaned in and put one hand on Gray's elbow, the other on the ball. "You're not following straight through."

"It *feels* like I'm coming through square."

"No, you're crooked." Reardon looked back at me. "Can you tell, Scotty?"

Future Hall-of-Famer Jeff "The Terminator" Reardon, who was closing in on the all-time save record, was asking me to corroborate his discovery of a mechanical flaw affecting Jeff Gray's splitter. *Are you kidding me?* He could've asked me to confess to a bank robbery I didn't commit, and I would have invented vivid details of the crime, then fabricated two witnesses placing me at the scene.

"Yeah, sure. I see it. Absolutely."

"O.K. Well, all right." Gray folded his arms, looked at his feet and sighed. "I'm with you."

"This video stuff can make a difference," said Term. "If I had this when I was younger, I would've saved forty every year."

"I've got to go work with Fish in the pen. Thanks, guys," said Gray.

Gray patted us each on shoulder then walked away.

"That must feel good, huh kid?"

I nodded.

"You're what…like twenty-two, twenty-three?"

"I'm twenty-two."

"Twenty-two and you're here, working with big league players."

"You won't hear me complaining."

"You keep watching the stuff that goes on in here and you'll know more than half the people in this place." Reardon paused, cleared his throat. "Does Lou know what you're doing down here?"

"I doubt it. I'd be surprised if he could finger me in a police lineup."

"I'm gonna let him know that all these machines back here saved a guy from getting hammered next time he goes out there, maybe even saved him from screwing up his arm."

"That would be great. Thanks, Jeff."

He paused, waiting for me to make the correction.

"Term."

He smiled and turned away.

Jeff Gray corrected the flaw in his delivery, and threw his splitter effectively in his next bullpen practice session, but he'd never throw another pitch in a big league game.

10

A Blowout Under Gray Skies

Jeff Gray was sprawled out in front of his locker, motionless, with his game whites on. Beside him, on one knee, was physical therapist Rich Zawacki.

"Jeff! Jeff!" he cried. When there was no response, he yelled, "Charlie, Joe, call the ambulance, Gray's down!"

Zawacki slid his hand down Gray's neck and felt for a pulse. Gray's face was pale, his eyes closed, and he had plump beads of sweat on his forehead. Zawacki leaned in, until his ear was inches from Gray's mouth.

"He's breathing."

Gray's eyes opened, wide and scared. He tried to pass words through lips that didn't move. His sounds were garbled, but purposeful, like those spoken to a dentist at unexpected pain.

"Jeff, don't try to talk," Zawacki said softly. He repeated his instructions to Charlie, louder this time, and again placed two fingers on the patient's neck as he counted the seconds on his wristwatch. Gray's eyes fluttered and closed. His neck went limp, tipping his head to the right.

"Too high, dammit," said Zawacki. Then, screaming, as if to declare the onset of panic, "Shit Charlie, where's that ambulance?"

Zawacki raised Gray's eyelids, revealing two brown marbles that sent shockwaves through the Red Sox trainer. Charlie and two paramedics rushed in and set up shop in the middle of the clubhouse. The players withdrew to the far wall and stood like children behind police tape at a crime scene.

In a blur of practiced movements, the paramedics lifted Gray onto a stretcher, buckled down his forehead and legs, then navigated him through the clubhouse to a waiting ambulance.

Rich provided a synopsis of his findings. "He's going to need a neurologist. Get him over to Beth Israel! Run every goddammed light! Go!"

I sat on the weight bench thinking about what I had just seen. Ellis came back—he'd seen Gray carried out the door—and when I described the details to him, his head dropped.

"But he'll be fine, right?" he asked.

"Don't know." I coughed, dry and forced, so I wouldn't have to talk. Several moments passed.

"They took him away in an ambulance."

"Was he talking?"

"No, he was just mumbling something, then he stopped and was quiet. Eyes shut, like he was dead."

Charlie told us that Jeff Gray was not dead, but aside from that we knew little else, just that it was bad and he was gone. I looked at Ellis as he bowed his head and knew he was thinking what I was thinking. *Jeff Gray's shot at the money left with him on that stretcher.* Ellis would move on to other teams and make millions with Colorado, San Francisco, and Cleveland. When it was too hot to play baseball and his back, knees, or hamstring was acting up, I wonder if Ellis ever thought about the day he saw Jeff Gray carried out on a stretcher.

The clubhouse atmosphere was reserved, but not morbid. This wasn't like a typical sports movie, where players sat at their lockers, arms folded, faces stoic and pensive, a touching piano melody playing in the background. Then, just before game time the grizzly veteran stands up and makes a moving speech imploring the team to compete, persevere, move on because that's what he (the missing person) would have wanted. No, it wasn't like that at all. This was reality, where drama was replaced with the task at hand, which was playing a game tonight against the Rangers.

I scooped some ice into my cup, pressed it against the soda dispenser, then leaned against the table and chewed on the ice chips. The radio was playing a local top-forty station. Catcher Tony Pena laughed at Luis Rivera, who shook his head as he pulled up a leg of his uniform pants. Greenwell was seated in the padded chair in front of his locker, a bottle of oil on the floor, his glove spread wide open on his lap. Naehring, Reed, and Lyons were watching *SportsCenter*. Jack Clark had his headphones on, reading the liner notes of a Crosby, Stills and Nash CD.

Physical therapist Rich Zawacki emerged from the trainer's room, poured a cup of coffee, and grimaced in my direction.

Zawacki was in his forties, had a runner's frame, and wore cheap glasses. His features hinted at a person deep in thought, and perhaps mildly annoyed.

"Any word?" I asked.

Zawacki held his response just long enough for me to know he didn't want to answer. "It's not good. He's not coming back anytime soon." Zawacki was about facts, nothing else.

Jeff Gray's street clothes hung neatly in his locker. Brown loafers toed the back corner; his beige socks were rolled tight and placed inside. There were no photos on the walls of the locker, just a small piece of paper taped to the inside, with a printed message and a small flower at the top. I wanted to get closer and thought more than once about strolling across the room to steal a glance (what did it say?), but his locker was remote, like it was in a different place, one full of fear and uncertainty and lost opportunity. I did approach that locker, but it was several weeks later, after it was cleaned out and restocked with a young man and his healthy body, a fresh start and high expectations. Only then would the gray shadows clear from that sliver of the clubhouse, would people begin to talk about him in the past tense, would Gray, thousands of miles away, begin months of grueling rehab, would the people who lived with him in the clubhouse begin to forget how he was here—resolute, methodical, fit—getting people out one day, out of baseball the next.

I called Kate from the phone out in the concourse to tell her about Gray's incident. She'd been watching a live broadcast from Yawkey Way, but all they'd said was that Jeff Gray was taken in for observation.

Just after 4:00, the reporters scurried in and chirped questions in all directions. They left the older players alone, mostly picking on the rookies who hadn't learned the art of looking busy, who were afraid to say no to a seasoned reporter, and who answered each question thoughtfully and in detail. Rookies didn't understand this was as good as handing an open invitation to the reporters that could have read something like this:

> I [rookie's name] invite you [insert reporter name] to ask me inane questions each and every day. I welcome being hammered with the aforementioned questions at any and all times, including, but not limited to: when I'm coming out of the shower, enjoying a pregame meal, talking with another player about game strategy, getting dressed, or watching *SportsCenter*.
>
> Even if I say I don't know or don't have an opinion, I authorize you to rephrase and re-ask until I give you the information, quote, or tidbit you require for your article. Should I break this contract, you are authorized to publicly flog my baseball skills, my effort or my attitude. At no time will I be allowed to refute anything you say.
>
> Signed,
> [insert player signature]

Today the reporters descended on Mike Gardiner, the pitcher I'd met a few weeks earlier, and they were asking him about Jeff Gray. I eavesdropped from my spot by the soda machine.

"Were you there when it happened, Mike?"

"No, I was not there and I don't know anything more than you guys do." He looked each of the three reporters in the eye, nodded as if to say "Good day," then stretched out his sock.

"Did you see it?"

Mike looked up, startled, as if he was driving alone and a freeloader suddenly sprang up from the back seat. "No," he said.

"So you didn't see any of it?"

"No."

How could he see it if he wasn't there?

"How's the mood in here?" asked the third reporter.

"Not too good, as you can see. Now if you'll let me—"

"Have you heard how he's doing?"

"No, I haven't." Gardiner looked at the floor. "Not recently."

"Who did you ask?" barked the first reporter.

"About what?"

"About Gray's condition."

"Well...I haven't asked anyone. I figured they'd make an announce—"

"Were you and Gray adversaries?"

"What? No. Why? Guys, I've got to get—"

"Can you tell us what the last thing was you and Gray spoke about?"

"I can't remember."

"Are you—"

Pena came over, squeezing through two reporters. *His savior had arrived.* "Gardy, I need to talk with you. Now."

Pena held Gardiner lightly by the arm, pulled him away from the reporters, and sat him down in a chair beside his locker. The reporters dispersed, hunting along the row of lockers for someone to give insights, quotes, or a vague reference they could parlay into a controversial story.

A balding reporter I hadn't seen before caught Brunansky's eye, but the veteran outfielder waved him off—politely but firmly—without uttering a word. Greenwell was next in line, so the reporter from the *Lowell Sun* slithered up to his locker, stood a few inches from his chair and asked, "Mike, you got a minute for a few questions?"

"Heck no. One of our guys has gone off to the hospital. I don't have time for no dumb-ass questions."

Greenwell had a temper, but played hard and cared about winning. He was honest and straightforward, but would pay dearly for the lack of courtesy he showed reporters, with subtle jabs in the papers and constant criticism of his defense, power, and arm strength. He hit .300 every year, ran out every ball, and trained like a prizefighter, but that's not what the reporters wrote about.

We pounded the Rangers that night, 11-6. The bullpen was shaky, giving up two runs late, but the game was over when the Sox scored ten runs in the third. Hits flew in all directions, foiling Oil Can Boyd's return to Fenway Park. The eccentric Boyd pitched for the Sox for several years, providing the media with dozens of bizarre controversies. In the Sox big inning, Carlos Quintana came up twice with the bases loaded, homering the first time, driving a double down the line the second time, resulting in six RBIs. Quintana's amazing feat tied a major league record for RBIs in an inning.

When Ranger catcher Mike Stanley doubled in the eighth, he stood with two feet on the bag, swiveled, and called out to the Red Sox second baseman.

"Jody, I heard about Gray goin' down. How is he?"

"Don't know," Jody said.

"Has anyone talked to him?"

"No. We don't know anything. Maybe we'll know more after the game."

Stanley shook his head, adjusted his helmet. "Tell him we're pullin' for him."

"Sure thing, Stano. Thanks for asking."

As the players filed in after the game, bushy-browed Dr. Pappas entered the clubhouse from his back office. He'd be the center of attention when the reporters arrived, providing general updates on Jeff Gray's condition, while side-stepping all specific questions like "When is he coming back?" or "What are his chances for a complete recovery?" Pappas was a rhetoric factory, a proud spire shimmering before the cameras, standing just tall enough to talk down to everyone, yet stopping low enough to blow smoke up everyone's ass.

The clubhouse door opened and the reporters rushed in like beagles sniffing for rubber sneakers, eyes wide and frantic, looking desperately for Pappas or Clemens or someone important, someone who could help fill the fifty lines of copy they needed to produce in the next three hours. Most nights, I enjoyed watching the first ten minutes of the post-game interviews as McAdam, Gee, Cafardo, Livingstone, and the rest charged in, jockeyed for position, and groveled for the attention of the millionaire athletes.

Many players simply wouldn't talk. Reliever Greg Harris shed his uniform as if it were on fire, changed back into his street clothes (without showering), and escaped before most of the players even tasted the post-game spread. Pena was known to spend fifty minutes sitting on the toilet, reading the newspaper cover to cover. Brunansky said, "Tony, you should thank those reporters for making you all worldly and shit! If it weren't for those pricks, you'd be one ignorant, constipated bastard!" Darwin iced his arm in the trainer's room for an hour. Charlie joked that Darwin's hatred of the reporters could lead to frostbite.

The Cave was a hideout for the media-averse. If someone threw a ball away late in the game and didn't want to answer silly questions, he'd be back with me. During a recent four-game losing streak, I had more than a dozen guys hanging out, and the reporters had no one to talk to. Jim Samia, a nervous man who served as the Red Sox media relations manager, came back and begged a few of the players to come out and answer a few questions.

"Tell them we're in an intense video-review session," said Greenwell.

Samia looked up at the screen, which featured a Playboy Playmates video Steve Lyons had brought in. "Strategy, huh? That doesn't look like any ballplayer I know," Samia said.

"Who said anything about ballplayers?" Greenwell clapped and looked around at his teammates, each of them mesmerized by the blond beauty on the screen.

"Dammit, Samia, this is some important shit!" Greenwell said. He turned and slapped rookie pitcher Kevin Morton on the knee. "We're *strategizing* on how we can get Morty some of this *Playboy* beef. This could take all fuckin' night!"

The room erupted with laughter while Greenwell stood up and slapped each guy a quick high-five, yelping and hooting odd sounds as he made his way around the half-circle of players. Samia retreated to the clubhouse empty-handed, with no one to speak to the media but Clemens.

Clemens' marriage with the reporters was a love-hate relationship without the love. Clemens stood by his locker every night and took his lumps for the team, as he used to say. He was expected to speak with the reporters, to answer questions about the team's performance or another player's actions. He considered it his duty as a leader. "Gotta go talk to the yard apes," he would say.

In Boston, people wanted to know everything they could about the team, so the reporters did their best to pry juicy details from every corner of the clubhouse, to construct half-truths from bits and pieces of information said by players relating to different events. Clemens once said, "Our defense struggled tonight, but they've been strong all year." This was presented to Reed and Boggs (who had recently committed errors) as, "Clemens says the defense struggled. Do you think your error tonight cost him a win?"

Reed was offended by the self-centered nature of these remarks, and he lashed out at Clemens. Alas! A problem was created where there was none. The reporter created controversy, which sold papers and made even a hapless team prickly and fascinating. That's just how it was in Boston.

Clemens actively sought out players as they arrived from the minors, or from another team, and counseled them on the perils of the Boston media. Gammons was better than Shaughnessy. McDonough is better than Ryan. Work with the guys from Providence or Worcester. Keep it short with anyone from the *Herald*. His evaluation was not based on literary merit, style, or grammar, but solely on the reporter's knack for turning things around, changing the angle on the facts, and interjecting opinions tainted by personal history. And most importantly, he said, "If you read something in the rags that I or anyone in here said about you, talk to them. Go see the man. Heck, they may not even 'a said it. But don't get back at them through the yard apes, that's the worst dang thing you can do. Wade and I did that and then there's no coming back."

The rift between the players and reporters was fascinating. Here were two groups of people, leaders in their professions, sparring each night; the players griping at negative portrayals, reporters pulling words from reluctant players and tying to put a special twist on the day's events. Darwin insisted that the writers didn't know anything about baseball. "How many games have you charted?" he once asked a reporter. "What the hell do you know?" In an informal week-long experiment, Matt Young once observed that following a victory there'd be three Red Sox articles in the *Globe*, but when we lost there would be five. "See, they love it when we lose!" he said.

I was torn between my co-workers and the writers I idolized. I thought Shaughnessy was a riot; Gammons was a legend. But there was no way I could embrace the reporters, not with all the hostility the players held for them. All I'd need was for one player to see me hob-knobbing with the yard apes, and my shot at inclusion would be gone. Though I saw Peter Gammons many times, I forced myself to stay away. It took everything I had to keep from rushing over to him and blurting out, "I loved you as a kid and you're great on ESPN! You know everything about the Sox!" As an insider, there were unwritten rules I had to follow; fraternizing with the reporters would have resulted in banishment.

Dr. Pappas announced Jeff Gray's condition: "There's no way to say when he'll pitch again." After the players heard that, everything was different, at least for today. They were willing to talk with the reporters.

"Gray was a good teammate."

"Hope he gets back here real soon."

"He was a fiery competitor."

"Jeff spoke about his family a lot."

"We miss him already."

Standard stuff taken from *The Definitive Cliché Collection: Baseball Edition*, Chapter 3: *Things to say when a player is hurt, demoted, released, or traded.*

Several players would visit Gray and speak with him on the phone, and those who did not threw out quotes to support Gray, and give his wife a few more press clippings to collect and share with the family.

Jeff Gray had had a stroke, his career was over. Could he come back? It was possible, sure. But when a player with marginal skills suffered even a slight twinge in his elbow, or a micro tear in his rotator cuff, it could take three mph off his heater, an inch off the break of his curveball or splitter. And that was enough to put a guy like Gray in Double-A. But this was much worse. It would be months before Jeff Gray could throw a ball across the kitchen table. He'd no longer battle pinch hitters. His challenges were in life's ordinary tasks: buttoning a shirt, eating with a fork, tying shoelaces.

11

Being Somebody

It was early August and Jack Clark was slumping. He wanted to see his at-bats from a few weeks earlier, when he'd smashed three home runs against Oakland. Jack only reviewed his good at-bats, never the bad ones. As we were watching Jack's last bomb, Tim asked me if I wanted to join him and Ellis at The Cask, a popular pub on the corner of Brookline Avenue and Williams Way.

"Sure, let me just finish up with Jack."

"I still have to shower, and Ellis is with the yard apes. It'll be a while."

"I'll wait out by the wives' lounge."

When Jack was finished, I shut everything down and stopped by Ellis' locker, where I found him seated with his elbows on his knees, mumbling to the reporters about his back pain.

"Mr. Burks," I said, "do you think the video system has helped you adjust to the various pitchers around the league?"

"Yeah, I'm hitting .260 instead of .240!"

Ellis turned to the reporters, "You know what, fellas, you should be talking to Cap'n Video. He's doing' some crazy stuff back there in the Cave. He's got something none of these other teams have."

The reporters looked at each other, then at me.

"Who are you?" one of them snapped.

"I'm Scott."

"What do you do here?"

I laughed, folded my arms. *Who was this guy? Heck, he wasn't even allowed to go the bathroom in the clubhouse.*

"Ellis, I'll be out by the wives' lounge."

Ellis saluted. "Gimme fifteen, Cap'n."

Joe was locking up the helmets in a small closet by the club-house door. "Mr. Cochran! I've been invited out for some beverages. Would you care to join us?"

He extended his hand, we slapped palms. "Wish I could. Chris is leaving early and Billy can't do it all by himself. I won't be outta here for another two hours."

"I'll have one for you. Bud?"

"Always. Have a good one, Cap'n. We'll do it all over again tomorrow."

I waited in a dark hallway connecting the players' parking lot to the clubhouse. Halfway down on the right, was a small room where the players' wives and children waited after the game. I recognized the voices of Michelle Reed and Debbie Boggs.

"…and Jody never swings at pitches like that. I think it's all this talk about his contract. Everyone's talking about how much he makes, and it's just not fair. Why do these people talk like that?"

"Hon, I don't think it will last much longer. He'll work it all out. Try not to worry so much. Let's go shopping tomorrow on Newbury Street. Wouldn't that be lovely?"

"I suppose."

"Tell the nanny you'll be out for lunch and have her bring the kids to the game. We'll have lunch, visit Ricardo's for a facial, and I need to pick up another pair of leather boots. I just love the red pair I have."

I shuffled further down the wall and bumped into Tom Sneed, who was seated in his folding chair in the dark.

"Sorry, Tom, didn't even see you."

"Hey, Scotty."

"What are you still doing here?"

"I'm always here, but I usually sit at the other end of the hall."

Tom was a co-op student at Northeastern who sat in a folding chair and made sure no unauthorized people entered the clubhouse. There were many jobs like this at Fenway, squatters who sat and did nothing for hours and hours. It had to be the worst job imaginable: sitting in a hall, protecting it from no one, counting the minutes until you could go home. Tom would watch players park their BMWs and Mercedes, listen to the organ music and cheering fans on the other side of the wall, but not even be able to watch the game on TV. After years of this, it could make you bitter, like the elevator guy who took patrons to the upper levels of Fenway. All night he took requests and pressed buttons. Tom brought his schoolbooks and did homework. He'd smile and tell you he was studying business and that he'd like to work for the Red Sox when he graduated. It was just a great place to be, he'd said.

Tom and I chatted until Ellis emerged, then I followed Ellis out to his car. He pulled a few fifties from his wallet, stuffed them in his front pocket, then placed the wallet on the front seat. He shut the door and said, "Let's go find Timmy."

"License?"

"Don't need it."

What was I thinking? It was unlikely he'd need identification to gain admittance to a pub a block away from where he roamed the outfield.

We went back through the dank tunnel towards the clubhouse and asked Tom if he'd like to join us. Said he couldn't, needed to study tonight. "I hope they hire you," said Ellis. "You work too damn hard."

Tom was hired by the Red Sox after he graduated from Northeastern. Several years later, Tom arrived at his desk to find "nigger lover" scrawled across a picture of his Caucasian girlfriend. He complained to Red Sox senior officials, but no investigation was launched. Not surprisingly, the culprit was never identified. Several months later he quit, then sued the Red Sox, but they reached a settlement before the case went to trial.

I smelled Tim's cologne several seconds before I saw him. He led us out the door of the clubhouse, around the concourse, down the third base line and through a rusty gate I'd never seen before. We stepped over a few scattered rakes and came upon another man sitting in a folding chair.

"Hi, Tim."

"Whaddaya say there, Henry?"

"Oh, you know…"

"Hi, Henry," said Ellis.

"Hey, Ellis."

Henry held out a brand new Rawlings baseball and a ball-point pen. Ellis took it, pulled off the cap and began scribbling his name.

"Henry, why do they got you sitting in the middle of nowhere in this chair?"

"Just following orders."

Ellis handed the ball and pen back to Henry.

"Thanks, Ellis."

We approached a green door; Tim grabbed the handle, kicked the bottom of the door three times, and it rattled open. Suddenly we stood on the sidewalk of Brookline Avenue. A crowd of college students sidestepped us and continued on their way.

"That was a damn labyrinth!" said Ellis. "I expected to see some rats and cheese and shit."

"Or some of those tall hedges," I added.

"Yeah, Clem's got rows of those at his house. You could get lost for a week in there," said Ellis.

"Maybe he should invite Hesky over and tell him there's a few dollars on the other side of the yard. We'd lose his eight wins and bullshit excuses," said Tim.

"This way," Tim said, pointing right. "Let's go."

Tim slowed down as we were in the middle of Lansdowne Street and came to a stop ten feet before the steps leading up to the front entrance. There was a line of people down the stairs, around the corner, and twenty yards down Brookline Avenue.

In the fours months I'd been around the players I'd learned to move slowly, not talk too much, and never stand with my hands in my pants pockets (it looked like you were at an eighth-grade dance). I was composed, but inside I was brimming with delight. If everything ended right here, this would be enough; I was having beers with Ellis Burks (who had gone 1-for-3 with a double and a walk) and Tim Naehring, the once and future shortstop. A beer would give my lips something to do, something to focus on other than *not* smiling, which required discipline and smooth shallow breaths.

The street-buzz shifted from erratic to controlled, and conversations became measured. People were staring at us. Tim and Ellis avoided eye contact with the crowd by looking out at the street, studying their shoes, and talking to me or each other. Tim wore a pleasant expression, on the edge of a grin, as if he'd met your mother for coffee and she'd shown him that baby picture of you with the spaghetti sauce covering your face.

Three months ago I was on the other side. If Kate and I had been at The Cask and seen Ellis and Tim, it would have been the highlight of the evening. Few would argue that the center-fielder for the Red Sox was more important than the governor. Hell, the lefty specialist out of the bullpen was more important than the governor. But I don't know what I would have done. Would I have approached Ellis and spoken with him? What would I have said? 'Nice hit tonight'? Would I have asked him to autograph my ATM receipt with the blotchy pen at the bottom of Kate's purse? Probably.

Someone from the line hollered, "Way to go tonight, Ellis!"

"Thank you," Ellis said quietly.

"How's the back feelin', Timmy?" a woman shouted.

Tim smiled, tilted his head for a moment and rotated his wrist slightly, which could be translated into: "It's O.K. I don't know how much longer I'll be out. I'm still upbeat. That's all I know right now. Thanks for asking." Tim had more style than anyone I'd ever met.

An attractive blond woman in a white Boston University T-shirt and black jeans approached Tim, pen in hand. "Tim, could you sign my shirt?"

He paused just long enough for her to feel awkward, recognize what she was asking, and rescind the request. But the woman stood her ground, never taking her eyes off Tim.

"Ellis, help me out here. This lady's got a ball-point pen. Can you tell her it's not going to work on a T-shirt, especially while she's wearing it?"

"O.K., I'll take it off," she said and grabbed the bottom of her shirt in her fists.

"Easy now," Tim said, like a policeman approaching an armed child.

Ellis stepped back and nodded his head. "Go for it, girl!"

"Ellis, you're killing me," Tim said.

Tim stepped past the woman and faced the crowd. "Can someone help us find a decent pen and some paper for this fine lady? We have a situation on our hands."

The crowd laughed; people frisked their pockets, tore apart their purses. This was the baseball player's version of "Is there a doctor in the house?"

Four pens, two pieces of paper, and a small notepad were raised high in the air, each person bidding to be selected by the handsome shortstop. Tim took the notepad and a pen from the crowd and returned to the overzealous BU student.

"Now, who can I write this out to?"

"Christina."

Tim whipped through his name, gently separated the paper from the pad, and handed it to Christina. She snatched it away, stuffed it into her bra, then took the pen and pad from Tim to write a message of her own.

She returned the pad to Tim. "I'm right down the street. Come by later," she said.

"Have a nice evening," Tim said.

As the woman returned to her place in line, Tim followed close behind and handed the pad back to its owner, Christina's note still attached. He mouthed a "thank you" to the woman and returned to Ellis and me.

The din of our presence had made its way through the line to the front door, where the bouncer motioned for us to come ahead. I started up the steps, but Tim and Ellis stood in their tracks. I turned back. "You guys coming?"

"Hold on," said Tim.

The bouncer called Tim's name, and he looked beyond me, waiting for an explicit invitation. "Tim, Ellis, come on in!"

If we had charged ahead and requested special treatment, it would have undoubtedly inspired rancor with some of the people waiting in line. As invited guests, we deflected negative sentiment to the bouncer and stayed in good graces with the fans.

At the door, Tim extended his hand. "Hi. What's your name?"

"Nick."

"Nick, Tim Naehring. It's a pleasure to meet you."

Tim didn't have to say his own name, but doing so gave the conversation normalcy and created a shred of equity between its participants.

Nick led us to a booth in the back corner of The Cask where our waitress, Holly, took our drink orders.

"What was that 2-2 pitch he got you on, Ellis?" asked Tim.

"Horseshit slider. Got so bug-eyed I popped the fucking thing up."

Tim laughed. "I thought you had him on that one. I've been like that… you see it coming and it looks so big and your backside flies out."

"Hey, what's the doc telling you about your back?" asked Ellis.

"I'm not getting–"

"Tim, hey would you mind…?" It was Nick the bouncer, standing by the booth, a pen and a piece of The Cask stationery in his hands.

"It's for my cousin, Anthony."

Tim took the office supplies from Nick. "How old is Anthony?" Tim asked.

"Um, he's eight."

"Sure. What position does he play?"

"Shortstop."

Tim began writing. "Good man."

"But you don't have to write it out to Anthony, just your name is fine. Then he can share it with his brother."

When Tim finished, he returned the pen and paper to Nick, who passed it to Ellis.

"Thank you."

"No problem," said Ellis.

"Take care," said Tim.

When Nick turned away, Tim shook his head. "Here we go."

Nick's public display brought Tim and Ellis to the attention of the patrons inside the busy bar. Just about every one a Red Sox fan who had attended the game. I'd learn later that Nick should have requested the autograph as we were leaving, improving the chances people would not immediately identify Tim or Ellis in a corner booth inside a crowded bar.

"So, what did Doctor Pappas say?" I asked.

"They're looking at the results out at UMASS Amherst."

"When will you know?"

"Hey, Tim!" A hefty man in jeans and Red Sox shirt appeared at our table, apparently wishing to greet the ball players.

"How's it going?" Tim said.

"You guys enjoying a beer?"

"Sure are."

"Hey Eddie, come here! I was right, it is Tim Naehring."

Eddie approached the table. "Hey, guys," said Eddie.

"Oh, sorry," said the larger man, "I'm Dan. This is Eddie."

We nodded hello to the two strangers.

"The guys here are just enjoying a beer. It's Ellis and Tim and…who are you?" The intruder paused, waiting for me to introduce myself.

"I'm Scott," I said.

"Are you somebody?"

"My mother thinks so."

Ellis grabbed my shoulder, then slapped the table. "That's good, Cap'n."

"Are you a player?"

"No, I am not a player."

"Oh."

O.K., could you go away now?

Tim stood up. "It was nice to meet you guys." He left the booth, not revealing his destination for fear he'd be followed to the restroom by grown men in Red Sox caps.

Eddie and Dan did not take this as a cue to return to their table, instead directing all of their attention to Ellis. They stood for several minutes at the end of our table asking questions about the team and the season. Was Clemens really a jerk? What was wrong with Jack Clark? Can we beat the Blue Jays? No. Nothing. Yes. It was unbearable.

The waitress appeared with our drinks, which Ellis used as an opportunity to end the interaction. "It was great talking with you guys."

"Sure thing, Ellis. Good luck."

I sipped my beer, then exhaled loudly. "That is so damn aggravating!"

"Oh, are you kidding me? Those guys were fine. There are much worse—people getting all animated and shit about some play you messed up three years ago. I don't even go out if I'm hitting less than .270! But now, it's fine."

Tim slid onto the bench opposite Ellis and me, picked up his beer, and took a long sip.

"Ahh! Now that's what I'm talking 'bout," he said.

"Our boy Scotty here's gettin' a little uptight."

Tim smiled, "What's up, Scotty?"

"It's annoying! How do you deal with these people?"

"They're not so bad. It just takes a little getting used to."

"But you can't even finish a sentence or someone's on you, asking you about Clem or the game or making some dumb-ass remark."

"This isn't the best place to go after a game."

"It's one thing to ask for an autograph for a kid, like Nick."

"Yeah, Nick, who we think has a cousin Anthony and some other cousin who he hasn't thought up yet."

"Huh? What do you mean?"

"I don't know Nick, and I'm not saying he lying, but nine out of ten times when someone asks you for an autograph for their kid or cousin or neighbor and they stop you from writing the kid's name, it's for them."

"Y'all are sneaky," said Ellis, "but we're on to your act!"

"I got nothin' to do with this. You know what, I'm not going out with you guys any more."

Tim and Ellis chuckled. "Too good for us now, Scotty?"

"Too normal. I just want to be left alone, drink my beer. I don't want to talk to these people. Next person that comes up to us I'm going to lay into and tell them to leave us the fuck alone!"

Tim shook his head knowingly, leaned in closer. "And tomorrow there'll be a story in the *Herald* about how Tim Naehring is the worst person in the world because he told off this fan who only wanted an autograph for his sick son. Then they'll be booing me every time I get up to the plate."

"O.K., you win." I finished off my beer with a long swig. "But you guys suck!"

I sat silently through the next three interruptions, fans who only wanted one autograph (it will only take a minute, thank you so much). *Was I like this?* Yes. Part of me still is. Why do we behave like this? There's this peculiar allure, the smell of fame, I guess; being close to them, meeting them, telling your friends about it, watching a game on TV and saying, "I met that guy." I couldn't deny I would have done the same thing: stood there like a buffoon, chirping small talk—him feigning interest in this random person who cheers for him, me building a contrived closeness with a man whom I've watched on TV several hundred times, hoping he'll talk to me, say something meaningful, ask me a question. As a fan, you think the players bask in this attention, enjoy talking with the fans, appreciate their affection, kind words and enthusiasm. At the park, yes, certainly. But at restaurants, the gas station, The Gap, the grocery store, on the sidewalk, in traffic, at the drive-thru, at every place all the time was excessive. It was way too much of a good thing. Invasion of privacy isn't just peeking through bushes to shoot pictures through half-open Venetian blinds; it's buddying-up with someone whom you've just met and will never speak with again by using his first name, slapping him on the back and asking pointed questions about his medical condition while he's standing at the latrine.

12

Red Hot Red Sox

Rookie Phil Plantier was called up from Pawtucket in early August, the day after they released Kevin Romine. I was at Tim's locker when Plantier bounced into the clubhouse, grabbed Naehring around the waist and lifted him in the air.

"Damn, Phil, put me down!"

Phil put him down and Tim adjusted his pants and shook his head in disgust.

"What's up buddy?" Phil said.

"You. Look at you, you're a house."

Phil pulled back his shirt, revealing an enormous bicep.

"That all you?" asked Tim.

"Of course, dude. Those steroids will shrink your pecker."

"Lord knows you can't afford that."

Phil smiled. "Ha! I forgot we were roommates. You know all my secrets."

"Phil, you know Scotty, right?"

"I remember seeing him last time. Video guy, right?"

"Yeah, that's me." We shook hands. "Welcome back. It's good to see you again."

"Timmy, they been messin' with me down there."

"Who?"

"Butch, all them coaches. Tellin' me to hit doubles and line drives. I don't care what the say down there about doubles, I want some dingers. Doubles get you sent back to Triple-A. You go deep, they keep you."

Plantier had a few at-bats the previous season and had been up for a cup of coffee in May before being sent down to make room for Mo Vaughn; this time he wanted to stay in the big leagues for good.

"So what's your plan, Phil?"

"Go yard."

"You're just gonna go yard, that's it? No new approach?"

"Yeah, I got a new approach. The guy throws the ball, I swing hard."

"Swing hard. That's the plan?"

"No, swing *really* hard. Swing my ass off. Come out of my shoes, you know what I mean?" He simulated a swing. "Bam!"

"Well I'll watch you from Instructional League. I'm heading there to do some rehab. Go get 'em."

Phil had shiny black hair, a dimpled smile, and the dreamy calm of a surfer. He was from San Diego, where they didn't understand baseball and would never have heard of Ted Williams had he not grown up there. Phil was a terrible fielder and didn't even enjoy playing baseball; he was here to make a few bucks, hang out with his friends, and drink beer. He was just five-ten and built like a tree stump. Phil's new hitting strategy, if you could call it that, paid off for him and the team, as he belted eleven homers in less than six weeks (a pace that would have put him at more than forty for the year). As he waited for the pitch, he crouched absurdly low, in what Manager Joe Morgan called "the toilet seat stance." When the ball was half-way to the plate, Phil uncoiled his body, sprung up from his crouch, and unleashed the full power of his oversized muscles on the ball. If the pitch had a few inches of late break on it, forget it; Phil missed it every time. He's the only person I've ever seen strike out five times in one game. Fortunately, he got enough straight heaters to keep his home run tear alive. Most teams had poor scouting and minimal access to satellite television, so each time we saw a new team they fed Phil a few fast-balls early in the count, learning the hard way that this free-swinging Californian would blast any fastball below his belt into the right field seats.

Phil and I became instant friends. We were roughly the same age—we grew up watching the same TV shows, seeing the same movies—only he didn't know anything about base-ball. Never watched it on TV. The veterans thought he was flaky, and the other rookies were serious and quiet and para-noid about getting sent down to the minors. Phil didn't give a crap, and because of that he played with a peaceful confidence bordering on laziness.

Phil came in early and sat back with me every day. He didn't want to see his at-bats; he just wanted to get away from the veterans who gave him shit all the time. I put on *Inside Edition* and he stayed until *Hard Copy* was over. He'd inter-rupt me constantly, telling me to look at this guy or that hot chick or this new movie coming out with Robert DeNiro, but I didn't mind because he was entertaining and I enjoyed his company.

When Plantier was called up, the Sox were in third place and out of the race. The reporters were merciless in their criticism of this under-achieving bunch. *Globe* columnist Michael Madden had soured on the team before the All-Star break. Shaughnessy was piling on the sarcasm. Bob Ryan scripted sophomoric monologues chastising Greenwell for everything from sliding head first into first-base to swinging at the first pitch. Matt Young was ridiculed by every other caller on the radio talk shows. The Sox were done; their diehard fans had left them for dead.

On Friday August 9, when the Sox visited Skydome to begin a four-game series with the first-place Blue Jays, they were eleven games out of first. The Sox hammered portly lefty David Wells and the Jays bullpen for twenty-one hits and twelve runs. The following night Greg Harris pitched a complete game masterpiece. In game three, Greenwell and Burks combined for seven hits, and Mike Gardiner pitched well enough to earn the win. In game four, with Clemens taking the mound, everyone was thinking sweep. But Clemens threw too many forkballs, and when he fell behind the hitters they sat on his heater and hit it hard. Clemens was chased from the game in the fifth as the Sox fell behind 7-5. But the veteran bats would not be denied. With two outs and a runner on in the sixth, Clark, Greenwell, Burks and Brunansky all punched singles, putting the Sox ahead to stay, and delivering a sweep of the shell-shocked Blue Jays. In the four-game series the Sox scored thirty-nine runs and sent a strong message to their Canadian rivals that they were back in the hunt.

While fans fumed over the dismal performance of last winter's free agent signings ($27 million on Clark, Darwin and Young), a handful of rookies and no-names with nothing to lose grinded out every inning and changed the course of the season. Kevin Morton and Mike Gardiner kept the Sox close and ate up innings, Plantier's homers energized the offense, and Hesketh was nothing less than spectacular. The veterans followed suit: Boggs played hurt and caught fire, hammering doubles off the wall like he did in '85; Reed was playing like an All-Star; Clemens was Clemens. The Sox won seven in a row in early September when it mattered most. When we hosted the Yankees for a weekend series in late September, New Englanders were brimming with confidence. The Toronto "Blow Jays" were crumbling: since August 7 they'd gone 20-21, while the Sox had gone 31-10.

The fifth-place Yankees had a lineup of burnouts and farmhands who stumbled their way into Fenway nineteen games out of first place. Clemens out-dueled Scott Sanderson on Friday night. On Saturday afternoon, Hesketh was brilliant for eight innings and Clark, Plantier and rookie Bob Zupcic all homered in a 12-1 pounding of the Yankees. Everyone believed we'd catch the Blue Jays; we were just a half game out of first place with two weeks remaining.

The final game of the Yankees series was played on Sunday, September 22. The Sox were down by a run in the eighth inning when Boggs singled and Reed walked. The autumn sun was fading. Darkness crept across the field, covering hitter Carlos Quintana in shadows. It was only fitting that the Q would be up when it mattered most. In spring training, he'd fended off Vaughn to keep his starting first-base job by putting up big numbers and playing great defense. When Morgan reduced his playing time after Vaughn's mid-season call-up, Quintana kept quiet and continued working hard, demonstrating a quiet dignity his teammates noted. Vaughn struggled, complained, had a shoving match with Greenwell, and strutted around the clubhouse until he was demoted to the minors. Carlos delivered a single, scoring Boggs with the tying run, sending Reed to third, and driving Fenway into delirium. Then a pitch bounced off Yankee Catcher Matt Nokes' glove for a passed ball, and Reed scored the go-ahead run.

In the top of the ninth, Jeff Reardon recorded two quick outs. The crowd noise shook the walls of The Cave as Reardon circled the mound preparing for the final out. A baseball game ends when it wants to, it has a pace and structure all its own, exempt from the tick of a clock's final seconds. Other sports mimic the forced hilarity of a New Year's celebration: Cheer now, the clock says. The Red Sox pitcher was moving this game to its inevitable conclusion. He looked into the catcher for the sign, but Pena didn't provide one, he just waved Reardon on, as if to say, "Just bring the heater, I don't care if everyone knows." The Terminator kicked his leg, huddled over his glove and exploded toward the plate. Roberto Kelly drilled Reardon's offering out of the park and a Dent-like silence filled Fenway. The Sox didn't score in the ninth. The Yankees won in it the tenth. Now, everything was different.

Roberto Kelly's homer ruined more than the final game of the Yankees series; it showered freezing rain on a red-hot team, fracturing the rhythm of effortless success, and making the team suddenly aware of who they really were, and what was missing. This edition of the Red Sox had a core of aging veterans, lifted into contention by a vulnerable gang of rookies and no-names. Although games remained and the statisticians assured us the Red Sox could still win the division, they were tired and inexperienced and lacked the resilience to recover, losing three of four in Milwaukee and letting the Blue Jays squeak into the playoffs.

Though they came up short, the Sox young talent had cut their teeth on a pennant race, and there was reason for optimism. Plantier was on the threshold of stardom, Gardiner proved he could be a solid number three starter, and most believed that Vaughn would return next spring, leaner and wiser, ready to reach his potential. Journeyman Joe Hesketh, who was a free agent at the end of the season, had pitched so well down the stretch that he was assured a big contract and a spot in the rotation. Reed, Boggs, Pena, Clemens and Greenwell would all be back in 1992. If Naehring and Burks were healthy and the Red Sox could just get one more starter—someone to do what Darwin and Young could not—they would be certain to make the playoffs. But we'd have to wait and see.

13

A Box of Balls and a Wad of Cash

After the crushing defeat at the hands of the Yanks, the team left for the road and I went home to watch the games from my couch. I imagined traveling to Baltimore and New York. What hotel do they stay at? What's it like walking into another stadium and working there for three days? I wanted to be with Boggs and Burks while they prepared for the game. It was during the final road series of the year, a weekday double-header in Baltimore, that I decided I had to travel with the team. What could be more thrilling than getting paid to see ballparks all over the country? The team's custom charter reportedly had a full-sized bar in the front of the plane, and personal TVs at every seat. They stayed at five-star hotels, dined at expensive restaurants, and got $75 a day for meals. In the weeks that followed I focused all my energy into making a case for bringing my contributions on the road. Convincing Lou Gorman and the financial tightwads upstairs to pay for a twenty-two-year-old computer guy to travel with the team would present its own set of interesting challenges.

Ending the season getting whipped by the Brewers was excruciating. The Sox had been officially eliminated earlier in the week, so no one cared. In the late innings, Greenwell slid out of the lineup and on to the bench, where he put on his jacket, stuffed his pockets with Bazooka bubble gum and sun-flower seeds, and paced from one end of the bench to the other. Brunansky wandered up to the clubhouse, lingered by the coffee machine, flipped channels on the clubhouse TV, and came back to harass me for a few innings. Pena went into the trainer's room and read a magazine from the third to the sixth. Burks sat at the end of the bench counting each out—bored, jittery, anxious to go home or to dinner—as the bench players and September call-ups whiffed on sliders in the dirt or popped out feebly to the infield. I don't know how the folks in Milwaukee and Detroit, who were eliminated by mid July, survived the season.

The final game of the season was played on the first Sunday in October; it's been that way since I was a kid. The players showed up late and most of the starters weren't in the lineup, so it was like a Triple-A game except for the size of the crowd and the BMWs in the players' parking lot. An outfielder named Bob Zupcic, who'd been called up a few weeks earlier, played for most of the game, rookie catcher Eric Wedge got a hit in his first major league at-bat, and a left-handed pitcher named Scott Taylor charmed the media as he explained how he threw eight different pitches.

When it was over I packed up the equipment, wiped down my worktable, and settled down to eat the post-game spread of chicken Marsala. I felt a hand on my shoulder and looked up to find Boggs, dressed in a dark blue Armani suit, standing behind me.

"I'm heading out," he said.

I put my plate on the floor and stood up.

"Thanks for all the help, Scotty," he said.

He glanced at his right hand, which was stuffed with a wad of hundred-dollar bills, and then looked at me. "A little something to say thanks."

I surrendered my hands. "Oh no Wade, you don't have to do that."

"I know." He raised his arm methodically, preparing to unload the cash like a backhoe moving sand.

I stepped back, slid flat hands in my beige khakis. "I'm just doing my job."

"It's okay, take it. We do it for a lot of the guys here."

I paused, considered the idea of leaving work with a pocketful of cash. *How much was in there, $500?* No, it had to be more. It was all hundreds, and five bills don't fold into a wad like that—you'd need seven or eight. He wouldn't even miss it, and who knows whether I'd even be back next year. What would my father do?

"I appreciate it, Wade, but I can't take your money."

He folded the wad into his suit pocket and shook my hand.

"But what would be really cool is a bat," I said. "I'd love to have one of your bats."

He returned a few minutes later with an unused bat. On it he had written: "To Scotty, Best Wishes, Wade Boggs."

On the way out I stopped by Phil's locker to exchange numbers. I wasn't sure if I'd be back, but I knew he would be; he was the next big thing.

"Scotty."

I turned around to see Clemens sitting at his locker.

"Hey, Roger."

"I wanted to talk with you about something."

"Sure, could you hold on one second?" I spun back and finished my conversation with Phil. He scribbled his San Diego number on a piece of paper and I stuffed it in my pocket.

"Clem, congrats on a great year."

"Thanks, Scotty. I appreciate it." Roger Clemens stood up, reached into his locker and pulled out a box of Rawlings baseballs.

"Want these?" he asked.

I lifted the top. Inside was a dozen unused baseballs, all signed on the sweet spot by the man who'd handed them to me.

"Sure, thanks."

"I figure you got people…"

"Yeah, and I always tell them no."

"We recognize that…you been here all summer and ain't bothered anyone about signing, and we appreciate that."

"Roger, this winter I was planning to add some features to that program I've been working on back there in the Cave."

"To help out us pitchers?"

"Yeah. Got any suggestions?"

"I sure as heck would like to see all my games in some better fashion than those pieces of paper the guys here scribble on the day before their start."

"Do you use the pitcher's charts?"

"Heck, half the time you can't read 'em, the other half of the time they're dead wrong. Double-D goes and gets himself some coffee and then just fills in the heater for all the pitches he missed. That's no help."

Danny Darwin, who was standing behind me at his locker, laughed. "You throw a lot of heaters Clem, it's as good a guess as any."

Clemens shook his head. "And Matty, he's even worse. I look at his charts and there's pitches on there I don't even throw!"

Matt Young joined in from his locker adjacent to Darwin's. "Come on now Roger, I think you're exaggerating just a little bit."

"Hell I am. Against Cleveland you had me throwing hooks to Alomar and the little guy Fermin. And there was a damn change-up on there! How's that gonna help me next time I go face them guys?"

"You don't need the charts Clem, just give the weasel some inside cheese."

Clemens shook them off and returned his attention to me. "See what I'm working with here?"

"I'll work on adding that type of charting to the computer program."

"Thanks, Scotty. See what you can do."

He extended his hand and I met it with a firm wrist. "Thanks for the balls, Roger."

I said good-byes to Ellis and Tim, stopped for a minute to chat with Joe, then reluctantly got in the car and drove home.

I didn't want this job to end. After being at the epicenter of one of the most tumultuous sports team in the country, I couldn't see myself in an office job, sitting in a cubicle all day. My expectations of what a job should be were hopelessly warped. On the drive home I deliberated about how I could become a part of the traveling group, thereby assuring my niche in the organization. I was convinced my ticket to travel lay hidden in lines of code yet to be written. The software needed to capture some missing information (when I knew what it was); only then could I become an essential part of the team's game preparation. Currently, all I did was show video in a highly efficient way to a few key players. I needed to get more hitters hooked, do something for the pitchers, and get the coaches involved. Then there was the issue of the cranky, ancient manager.

After dinner, I sat at the kitchen table and decided to plot my course. Kate was out running errands, and the TV was off, so it was silent in our one-bedroom apartment except for the clicking sound of the radiator and the muffled TV across the hall. I began to scribble ideas on the yellow-lined pad in front of me, tearing through page after page as I recalled the experiences of the last few months. I was nothing during those months if not a good listener; I committed to memory the details of every important comment and conversation. As players viewed their at-bats, I kept detailed notes. The key was to be able to translate those notes and observations into new features.

14

Cracking The Code

Manager Joe Morgan was fired a few days after the season ended, a favorable move for me, given that Morgan despised computers and had no interest in what I was doing. Luis Rivera mocked Morgan's slow Boston drawl. Jack Clark didn't get special treatment, so he ripped Morgan in the papers. Greenwell thought he was senile. Morgan lost his players' respect by ignoring proven game strategies (advancing the runner with a bunt, righty-lefty match-ups), instead relying on his flaky hunches in critical game situations. He'd lost control of the clubhouse by ignoring the rookies, failing to respect the veterans, and not keeping an eye on what was going on around him. I worked in his clubhouse for five months and I had never spoken to Joe Morgan.

Butch Hobson was immediately named the new Red Sox manager. Hobson was a hard-nosed third baseman when I was a kid, a football player from Alabama stuck playing baseball for a living. He purported to coach his teams á la his beloved Bear Bryant, with tough love. Butch's teams played hard, never game up, and respected the game. I didn't know how this boot-camp approach would work with guys like Young and Brunansky, but I was hopeful I could use this opportunity to build a strong relationship with the new coaches and improve my standing in the clubhouse.

Throughout October and November, I worked with my father to improve the software I'd used during my inaugural season. Currently, all the software did was control the video-disc player; the computer was little more than a convenience. During these months, we explored its potential for storing and retrieving scouting information. I designed most of the screens—how they would be laid out and what they would contain—and my father worked on the background calculations that would provide all the critical data we thought the players needed. He taught me the programming as he did it, so I'd be able to take it over, improve it, make changes. We were developing something based on what I had learned, with no guarantee that it would provide the players any advantage in preparing for a game. The main feature addition was creating an easy way to chart pitch type, pitch location and where the ball was hit. If we could do this, Clemens would be on board and the other pitchers would follow. The work was tedious and not particularly enjoyable, but I was unemployed and therefore highly motivated.

Pitcher Mike Gardiner, who had decided to spend the winter in an apartment downtown, proved to be a key resource. He drew pictures of what the screens could look like and I implemented exactly what he suggested. First I created a small screen to enter the pitch type, with buttons containing two-letter abbreviations for all the major pitches: FB (fastball), CV (curveball), SL (slider), CH (change-up), FK (forkball), CT (cutter), SI (sinker). The next screen, used to capture pitch location, looked like a tic-tac-toe board with labels in each square. It was from the pitcher's viewpoint, so clicking the lower right-hand square, for example, would enter in the letters "LI", for "low inside." We made an alternate grid for use when a lefty was up, in which case a pitch in the lower right corner of the grid was "LO," for low and outside.

The third window was for the result of the pitch. It could be ball, strike swinging, strike looking, single, double, triple, homer, wild pitch, hit-by-pitch, fly out, ground out, or passed ball. If the ball was put in play there was a fourth window which contained a picture of a baseball field. We sliced the field into fifteen different areas and we'd click on an area of the field to input our selection. Gardy figured this data would allow us to create defensive positioning diagrams.

Compiling this data for a season would allow us to analyze critical game situations and eventually provide scouting reports to the coaches and players. First I had to learn the norms. For a good hitter, pitch location and pitch type dictated where the ball should be hit. For example, hitters generally pulled an inside fastball in the high eighties. Fastballs away should be hit up the middle or the other way. Change-ups should be pulled, because the hitter is out in front of the pitch. Sinkers were hit on the ground. Forkballs were generally missed or taken for a ball, unless it was a thigh-high hanger, in which case it was hammered. What remained was to sift through and locate tendencies outside these norms, then pass these findings on to a coach or player who could capitalize on them, by either modifying our pitcher's pitch sequence or making defensive adjustments. I learned that baseball is about making adjustments. Clemens told Gardy that Don Mattingly always took the forkball with two strikes, so in his next at-bat, Clemens threw him five consecutive forkballs, his way of breaking the pattern and getting into Mattingly's head.

All hitters had their own unique traits and approached hitting in their own way. Was a guy pulling the outside fastball? Was he getting a lot of hits on change-ups, which might identify him as a guess hitter, who was sitting on one pitch? Did he pull his hands in and try to shoot the inside fastball the other way? How often did the hitter swing at the first pitch? Was he a bad-ball hitter, like Kirby Puckett, who often got hits on balls outside the strike zone? Did he hit the slider better than the curveball? Would he change his approach, shorten his swing, and try to go the other way with two strikes? There would be hundreds of scenarios to inspect, countless pitch sequences to consider.

Using the computer to track each confrontation, Gardy believed we could uncover tendencies. The sequence of pitches thrown by Dave Stewart, Jack Morris, and Scott Sanderson was not whimsical or random; it was a calculated plan of attack. If we could crack the code of the league's top pitchers, our hitters might be able to expect a certain pitch in a certain situation. If you told a big-league hitter he could sit on one pitch, chances are he'd crush it. The opposing pitcher would quickly alter his pattern, but we could leverage these windows of opportunity to give our hitter an edge in a key situation. Some of the coaches in Oakland and Chicago reportedly scoured through pitching charts to uncover these tendencies, but with the power of a computer we could locate hidden nuggets quicker, and find some they might overlook. Our system was interactive. For example, we could show the hitter an on-screen report revealing that Baltimore pitcher Mike Mussina liked to throw his change-up in 2-0 counts, and then click on that 2-0 pitch, or any other pitch. The hitter could review the supporting evidence and also re-familiarize himself with Mussina's arm action and ball movement. But first we had to get the program working so the data could be input, retrieved, and analyzed.

My plan for next season was to chart the opposing pitcher on the computer during the game, capturing every pitch type, location and result. Right now, my charting accuracy was less than fifty percent, but Gardy or Tim would help me out until I improved. Last season I'd studied nearly seventy thousand pitches and I hoped with another hundred thousand I could get where I needed to be. The Red Sox pitchers could use "The Pitcher's Edge" program instead of the paper charts they scribbled on the day before their scheduled start. Then Clemens or Hesketh or Darwin would be sitting with me charting the Red Sox pitcher on a laptop computer while I charted our opponent. I could ask questions, pick their brain, and learn the nuances of the game.

The hitter's program also needed to be improved. I called Tim a few times at his condo in Cincinnati looking for suggestions, but I never heard from him, so I called Phil. He wasn't a student of the game, but at least he was accessible.

"Shit, buddy, I got no idea what you're talking about," Phil said.

"I'm talking about your approach."

"My approach?"

"Yes, tell me what you need to do to get ready for a game."

"Sober up."

"C'mon, Phil, I'm serious."

"So am I."

"Yeah, well that's not gonna help me. I don't think you get this. There's no guarantee I'll be back next year. Lou hasn't been returning my calls, and I haven't even met the new coaches. I've got to take this thing to the next level or I could be out on the street, or worse, in some damn office pushing papers." I shifted the phone to my other ear. "Phil, are you there?"

"Yeah, I'm here. Can you believe this shit with Magic Johnson? I cannot believe the guy has AIDS."

"Phil, that happened like two weeks ago."

"Well, I just heard about it. It's crazy out there."

"Phil, can you help me out with this program?"

"You know, I was talking to this guy at the gym who knows a lot about computers, and he was saying that you should sell that program to all the other teams."

"Yeah, you told me that before."

"So why don't you?"

"Because I don't want to. I work for the Red Sox."

"Are you sure? Sounds like they're doggin' ya. You need to be a free agent, make yourself some coin. I'll get you a good agent, and you'll be raking it in."

"O.K., sounds good. Get me your agent's number and I'll give it a go." *What the hell is he talking about?* "Now, Phil can you tell me something about how you prepare for a game? What do you want to know about the pitcher you're facing that night?"

"Nothin'."

"Nothing? Nothing at all?"

"Heck, no."

"What about his pitch repertoire?"

"His what?"

"Don't you want to know what he throws?"

"No, I don't care. Get a good heater and just swing hard. That's all there is to it. Get yourself a fastball and give it a rip, just in case you hit it."

"What about in the outfield? How do you know where to play?"

"There are bare spots in the grass out there, one for lefties, one for righties. I just stand there. Sometimes, if some loud guy's yelling at me, or the game's kind of boring, I forget to move to the lefty patch. But I don't think anyone notices, at least no one's ever said anything to me."

What if there are more guys like Phil, guys who don't care about strategy? I squashed my panic before it started. No, there's no one quite like Phil.

I worried about the direction our project was taking. Were we capturing, recording, and filtering the right information? If Gardy was wrong, this could be a disaster, a complete waste of time, but I had to continue to work on it. I had to try. If I could improve the software, I could grow this video position into a full-time job, maybe even something more. I wanted to be invited back for the 1992 season, and I wanted baseball to be my career. The small taste I'd had of life in the big leagues made me thirst for more, yet I was unnerved by how little I knew about the game. Only by building this software could I make significant contributions and become a valuable resource to the team. Then I'd be around the players for one hundred and sixty-two games, I'd be their confidant, and they might teach me all the subtle strategies behind this game. From there, I could do anything.

15

The Rocket's Laptop

Roger Clemens was awarded his third Cy Young in a landslide. Two days later, he left a message on my answering machine.

"Howdy, Scotty, Clem here…ahh, could I talk to you about picking up a laptop? I've got a lot of personal stuff and some notes I keep about the umpires I'd like to get on a computer. And you said you're adding to that program to help out the pitchers. Anyway, give me a holler at 209-555-2121. I'll be in Katy most of the day. Be sure to tell the folks you're caller twenty-one."

I fumbled for the phone. *I'll call him right now. What time is it? Eleven o'clock, too late. Tomorrow, first thing.*

Was it really Clemens? It couldn't have been. It must've been Phil, the bastard! I played back the message again, then a third time. It was Clemens. I took the tape from the machine, labeled it with red marker, put it in the drawer next to the silverware. Tomorrow I would go to Radio Shack for a new tape.

When I called at 9:30 the next morning (8:30 A.M. Central time), a woman answered the phone. "Roger Clemens Foundation."

I told her my name, that I was returning a call from Roger.

"O.K., well I'll take your number and have him get back to you. He's traveling to Houston today for a special event."

"But, he told…"

"Sir, if that is all, I'll take your number and pass it along to Roger."

"He told me he'd be in Katy most of the day."

Silence.

"Sir, is there anything else?"

"Caller twenty-one."

"Hold on, I will connect you."

Roger was friendly, but brief. He needed a laptop and asked if I could pick it out for him.

"O.K., I'll do it today."

"So send it along to me. FedEx it and put a note in there with your address and whatever the fee is for your time."

"Roger, you don't have to pay me. I'll send you the receipt so you can pay me back for the computer."

"Get the best one they have."

Thirty minutes later, I was at CompUSA looking at Macintosh laptops. "I want the best one you have," I told the salesman.

No bartering, no comparison shopping. It was very liberating.

"Are you sure?"

"Yes."

He brought me to the edge of the supply room, disappeared for a moment, and returned with a shrink-wrapped box.

"Here it is, the new Macintosh PowerBook. Best one they make. Fast, big screen. You can't buy anything better."

"Sounds good. I'll take it."

A man and his teenage son stood by the printers, half listening to our conversation.

"Don't you want to know how much it is?"

"No. Doesn't matter."

"It's $5200."

"Fine." I leaned in to accept the box from him. "I appreciate your help."

The salesman's eyes were narrow, his expression frozen. I took a few steps toward the register.

"Sir…" the man said.

"Yes."

"One last thing. There is a twenty percent restocking fee if you return the computer for any reason."

"Even if I don't open the box?"

"Yes."

I did my best to maintain the charade.

"O.K. If that's the rule."

I set the computer down on the register. The clerk was staring at me. He probably didn't see this every day; a guy in his early twenties in jeans and a ratty leather jacket buying a five-thousand-dollar computer.

"These laptops just came in," he said. "It's a nice one."

"Yeah, it looks O.K."

"What do you plan on using it for?"

"I'm not sure." I reached for my wallet. "So what's the total going to be?"

"Would you like to buy our extended service plan on this, sir?"

"No, thanks."

"O.K., then, so the total comes to $5210. How would you like to pay for that?"

Then it hit me. *How was I going to pay for this?* Fear chilled my body like a morning plunge into a mountain lake. I felt the clerk's eyes upon me, turned to see three other customers in line, including the father and son who'd watched me earlier. I had two credit cards, Discover and MasterCard. Discover had a credit limit of $3000, a current balance of more than $1000; MasterCard had a limit of $2500 and a balance of $500. If I split the bill between the two cards I still only had $4000. My performance ended abruptly.

"You know what," I leaned in, lowered my voice, "can you put this on hold, and I'll come back for it in a few days?"

"We can hold it for twenty-four hours, unless you put a deposit down, then we can hold it for two weeks."

"How much of a deposit is required?"

"Twenty percent."

"O.K., I'll do that."

"But if you decide not to purchase the computer, you'll be charged a restocking fee of 10 percent."

"There's a restocking fee?"

"Yes.

"Even if it doesn't leave the store?"

"Yes, even if it doesn't leave the store," he said, an octave higher with each word.

"That doesn't make any sense."

He strummed his fingers on the box. "When you put it on hold, it's taken off the shelves. We no longer have the opportunity to sell it."

How far I'd fallen. Ten minutes ago I could've been considered an eccentric; a twenty-something computer mogul strutting in and nonchalantly buying an absurdly expensive computer. Now I was bickering with a clerk about a return policy spelled out in signage over every check-out line.

"Sir, that's our policy. Now, if you're uncertain of your purchase, we have many other, less expensive computers."

Ouch.

"I'll do the layaway thing."

"That'll be $1040."

I handed him my card.

"On Discover," he snarled, revealing a hideous grin. "Hmm."

American Express Gold or Platinum (or any associated precious metal) is the card of someone who buys a $5200 computer. I'd been exposed as a pretender, busted for masquerading as an important person, and my Discover Card was Exhibit A in the case against me.

The Mustang hummed patiently as I sat in the parking lot, stared at the windshield and considered my options. Should I call Clemens and ask him to send me a check? No, that would make it look like I either didn't trust him or didn't have the money to cover the computer (true, but too embarrassing). If he sent the check in advance, would he be afraid I'd run with it? I couldn't face the possibility of rejection, of some relative or trusted friend admonishing Roger on the risks of sending a $5200 check to some seasonal employee he'd known only a few months. I'd somehow get the money, buy the damn computer, and send it to him.

The friendly folks at Discover wouldn't raise my credit limit because my income hadn't changed, I'd carried a balance every month for the last twelve, and I'd had a late payment in November. Call back in six months, they said. MasterCard gave me an extra $500, but that still wasn't enough. Kate was my only hope; she had $1400 in her savings account. Thank goodness I'd had her listen to the tape, or she may have thought I was masking a drug habit. Borrowing money to get Roger Clemens a computer was a preposterous premise.

The next day at CompUSA Kate and I stood in the customer service line for twenty-five minutes before a salesman retrieved the machine from the back shelf and sent us on our way. I'd paid the $1040 down payment, so the balance due was $4160, which I divided between three sources: Kate's $1300 check (we wanted to leave $100 in the account so Kate didn't have to close it); a charge on my Discover; and a charge on MasterCard. It was terribly ugly.

On Tuesday I FedEx'd the computer to Clemens' residence and included the receipts with the packing slips. I called and left a message for him Tuesday afternoon to make certain he received it, and asked when I could expect the check. On Wednesday I went skiing at Gunstock. Thursday morning there was a knock on the door. A FedEx man handed me a package from The Roger Clemens Foundation containing a thank you note from Roger and a personal check I couldn't cash.

The check remained in my wallet for three days; I didn't want to give it up. Finally, I called Clemens and left a message explaining the problem I'd seen with the check and asking him to send a new one. Someone from the foundation called and apologized; the Clemens' were on vacation, and they'd have Mr. Clemens write a new check as soon as he returned.

In December, Lou's assistant Ann Marie phoned, and in a voice as cordial as chalk dust, she told me to be at the clubhouse at one o'clock the following day. She did not ask if I had plans or if the short notice was going to be a problem.

"Butch Hobson is in town with the coaching staff. You will give them a demonstration of the video system." With that, she hung up.

I knew that Butch and his coaches' reaction in this meeting would determine whether I was renewed or released. A lonely chill had settled into me during the last few months; tomorrow it would be gone. I watched the evening sports update with renewed interest. I knew they'd have a few sound bites from Hobson; Boston sports fans are always interested in hearing anything about baseball. I sat on the couch, giddy from the release of three months of stress, yet weakened by the thought of a meeting in little more than 12 hours that would alone determine my future with the Red Sox.

Hobson stood proudly in front of the camera with snow white hair and a plaid checked sports jacket, answering the reporter's questions in broken English masked by his thick Alabama accent.

"Who will start at first? Are you leaning toward Vaughn or Quintana?" the reporter asked.

The baseball season was three months away, the Celtics were playing better, and the Bruins were in second place, but the locals still cared more about the Red Sox.

"Well Sir, I know Carlos has a quick bat and he been strong with that glove. But Mo…well, he's a big fella. Yes, a big fella. He can drive in a lot of runs for us. We'll have to get him in that lineup somehow."

Butch had not met his players, hadn't managed a single game, but he'd already committed a major gaffe: he answered an important question in the media before consulting his players. Carlos Quintana was at home in Venezuela, but he'd soon get word from his friends in New England his new manager favored the rookie Vaughn. The new manager had hardly seen Quintana play. This was the beginning of Hobson's rocky ride; Butch often did not know when he'd said or done something wrong, so he repeated his mistakes. Someone should have told him.

16

The Meeting

When the alarm buzzed at 5:30 A.M., I was wide awake staring at the ceiling, feeling as if I had never slept. I took one bite of an English muffin and tossed it in the trash. I showered, dressed, and sped into Boston to meet with the new coaching staff of the Red Sox. As I turned on to Yawkey, I tapped the horn and waited for Al to open the gate, then pulled the car down the concourse, past the clubhouse and parked in front of the beer stand.

It was just before eight and Joe wouldn't be in until after nine, so I walked up a short ramp toward the field and found a seat along the first base line. Abandoned by players, seasonal staff and fans, Fenway was desolate. A thick film of dirt occupied the lower box seats. The tarpaulin sealed off the infield, protecting the precious soil from the perils of winter, as the grass counted the short daylight hours until it could feel the tickle of cleats and the warmth of the sun.

The wind was sharp, the sun weak, and my eyes found the distant stare of deep thought. I found great comfort and peace in these solitary moments in Fenway Park. There were no vendors, no balls or bats, no movement of any kind, creating an eerie stillness over this historic plot of land in this busy city. It was the absence of all sources of interruption—save a few geese flying in formation over the center field score-board—that made my thoughts clearer. Unwieldy troubles were broken into coarse pieces, smoothed, then resolved; smaller, nagging worries simply dissolved. Though time has shuffled its contents, when I remove the lid on my shoebox of Fenway memories these quiet moments are always on top.

For Red Sox Nation, baseball was over until spring. Nowhere was this more evident than in Fenway Park in the morning hours of an oncoming New England Winter. But I was no longer an ordinary member of Red Sox Nation; I was on the inside and fighting to stay there.

I assessed the crew that would decide my fate. Crusty Don Zimmer, the manager of the '78 Red Sox, wasn't likely to be interested in a computer video system, so I planned to direct my efforts at the others and avoid any egregious errors that could expose my baseball ignorance. Manager Butch Hobson was "old school," and in all likelihood computers weren't part of his managing strategy. Base coaches Al Bumbry and Gary Allenson, both intelligent, hard-nosed players, might favor the idea, but would likely be suspicious of a non-former player operating the system. Pitching Coach Rich Gale was bright and articulate, and seemed open to new ideas. New hitting coach Rick Burleson could be the swing vote; if he was in one of his notorious bad moods I could be in the unemployment line. It didn't seem fair to have my career, and the course of my life, hinge on a brief meeting with six strangers who were tired and ready to go home, who didn't know anything about what I'd done the last four months of the season, how much I'd learned, and how much impact I could have next year. When the chill in my fingers spread up my arms to my shoulders, I shivered, stood up and exhaled through chattering teeth.

It was just before nine and I knew Joe would be ready for another cup of coffee, so I picked one up for him at the Batter's Box, entered through the unlocked clubhouse door and sat down at the gray table. I was flipping the channel to ESPN when he emerged from the manager's office.

"Captain Video!"

I handed him a coffee. "Big day today, Joe."

He peeled back the plastic tab on the lid, raised the cup to me in appreciation. Joe never said thank you, not that I'd ever heard.

"Oh yeah, Scotty. The big man will be here around two. Been cleaning out all of Morgan's old shit. You'd think he'd been here thirty years. Gotta have the office ready when he gets here, or Lou will get all bent out of shape."

"Hope he's a good guy."

"I've got some dirt on him, Scotty. Met the man a few times myself in Winter Haven." Joe spoke slowly, measuring every word. Talking slower stretched conversations, made the day go by easier. "Heard he's a good shit."

"That's good to know."

"Yeah, but some of those coaches could be high-maintenance." Everyone was ordered in Joe's mind by how much they required of him. "Burleson is supposed to have some personality issues."

"I heard that," I said.

"Someone told me he was so bad that it was damn near a medical condition."

Joe laughed and shook his head.

"Must've been Marzano. That sounds like something he'd say."

We sat at the old steel table and talked for a half-hour about how a few of Joe's assistants had spent the last two weeks driving Jack Clark's motor home out to the West Coast. Clark paid for gas and hotels, gave them each a few hundred in cash, and then let them stay at his beach house for the weekend. He lived right on the water and Clark's wife made them waffles and eggs Benedict. After three days of eating like kings and drinking Heineken on the beach, Jack sent them home on a first-class flight to Boston.

The video area was dusty and dark. I changed a few bulbs and stacked up the tapes and laserdiscs into neat piles. I wiped down everything with a moist towel because I knew Lou would want it all cleaned up for the new coaches. When I was confident that everything was functioning properly, I ran through a few laserdiscs and found some examples to show the staff. The meeting would hinge on my ability to explain the system to "baseball men" of varying intelligence. Some would get it instantly and have suggestions, and others would shut it out and badmouth it after they left. I had to show them the benefits without intimidating them; I had to impress them with my baseball knowledge without making it seem contrived. I had never met these guys, so I'd have to get a quick read on each personality and work the guys who seemed interested. My future depended on it.

I had the TV on, my feet on the table and a plate of pizza in my lap when I heard some chatter down in the clubhouse. I gathered myself together, took a deep breath, and headed through the exercise room to meet the new manager and his coaching staff.

As I turned the corner into the clubhouse, I nearly bumped into old timer Johnny Pesky, who was leaving the restroom.

"Hi, Scotty!" Pesky said.

"Hey, Johnny," I said, extending my hand. "It's great to see you."

Johnny Pesky was one of Ted Williams' closest friends, a player and former manager for the Red Sox in the '40s and '50s. Well into his seventies, he still had a full head of grey hair, bright eyes and a firm handshake.

"You here to show these guys some of that fine work you do back there?"

"You got it, Johnny. I hope they like it."

"Aw, don't worry about it. I'll have a word with Zimmer and we'll work something out."

I didn't doubt that Johnny would speak to Zimmer, but I wasn't sure it would do much good. Johnny didn't really know what I did, so he'd have limited ammunition to use in building a case to Zimmer for my continued employment.

"Thanks, Johnny."

Pesky slapped my back, moved his hand up to my shoulder and squeezed.

"You're a good kid, Scotty. You'll be around."

Johnny Pesky's optimism lit up even the darkest corners of Fenway. Johnny traveled with the team when he felt up to it, sat in the dugout on occasion, and still hit fungoes to Greenwell and Burks. He rarely spoke of his days setting the table for Ted Williams, "the greatest hitter who ever lived," choosing to live in the present unless prodded into storytelling. He wore his number six uniform with pride.

Earlier in the year, Greenwell said, "Johnny, one day I'll be as old as you and I'll be coming back telling all the young guys how close we came to winning in '86 and '90 and beggin' them to win the goddammed World Series so I can go home and play golf and not have to hang around the park waiting for the damn Curse of the Bambino to end."

Johnny smiled and said, "No, Greenie, you'll do it before then. You'd better, for Christ's sake. I don't know how much time I have left."

I waited as Johnny continued across the room and greeted the new coaches. They all wore stern faces, wool overcoats, and designer suits. I stood in the doorway at the other end of the clubhouse, waiting for them to make their way to the Cave. Joe was showing Hobson the manager's office, and the coaches were milling about their lockers discussing their flight arrangements out of town.

The tallest man, whom I knew to be pitching coach Rich Gale, stepped forward and extended his hand. Don Zimmer and Rick Burleson were slightly behind and to his left.

"I've been waiting all day to meet you," Gale said. "I've got a lot of ideas I'd like to talk to you about!"

We shook hands and then walked toward the back room, the coaching staff in tow.

Kate was lying on the couch, talking on the phone, the long white cord twirled around her arm three or four times. She wore blue sweat pants and a Red Sox T-shirt.

"Sorry, Scott just walked in, I'll have to call you back. O.K., bye."

She hung up the phone and jumped up from the couch. "How did it go?"

"Oh, hi." I walked into the kitchen.

"How was it?"

"Fine."

"Did everything work?"

"Yes."

She burst into the kitchen and hovered over me as I opened the refrigerator and grabbed a can of Mountain Dew. I walked into the living area, took off my shoes, then sat on the couch.

My insouciance brought her to the boiling point. "Scott! Don't do this! Tell me what happened! Now!" She was clenching her fists, waving her arms up and down.

"Kate, it was amazing. I don't think it could have gone better."

"Really? Oh, my God, I was so nervous I couldn't do anything. I just called everyone I knew trying not to think about it and then I'd say, 'Yeah, Scott is meeting with the new coaching staff today,' and then I'd be worse off than I was before trying to tell everyone how important this meeting was and about your contract and maybe traveling…"

"Geez, it's hard to get a word in here." I grinned, folded my arms.

"Okay, okay, so come on, tell me!"

"Well, I had an English muffin for breakfast and then I got into the car—"

"Tell me before I tackle you and torture it out of you."

"Maybe I'll hold out." I rubbed my chin. "Sounds interesting."

She growled at me and put her hands on her hips.

"Okay, okay!" I hugged her and whispered in her ear. "It was perfect. These guys are young, they're energetic."

"How so?"

"Well, they use computers, they have ideas. I don't feel like I'm jamming the computer down their throats. They're all over it."

"Really?"

"They liked the video...using the laserdisc and all that stuff. They said it looked great, especially for hitters who were struggling. And they had ideas for adding in different camera angles. And you won't believe what Gary Allenson said."

"Who's he?"

"That backup catcher I was telling you about. Mugsy, from when I was a kid."

"Okay, yeah..."

"Well, he's the bullpen coach with these guys and he says, 'How can we see what pitches they're throwing to our guys? Can we tie this together with our charts?'"

"Now isn't that what you've just been workin' on?"

"Yes! It was like I wrote a script for them to read!"

The coaches were floored when I showed them how the game could be easily charted on the computer using the program we developed; no more paper charts that no one ever looked at.

"Does anyone else have this?" pitching coach Rich Gale asked.

"No. I developed this for the Red Sox."

Gale turned to Gorman, who was beaming. "Lou, where'd you get this guy? He's the secret weapon!"

Towards the end of the meeting, which lasted nearly two hours and caused two of the men to miss their flights, Rich Gale turned to me and asked, "Do you work all the games?"

"No, last season I worked only the home games."

"Lou, this guy's gotta come with us," Gale said. "If we're going to do this we need to have it everywhere. Spring training, road games, everything."

And so it was decided. Rich Gale said I should travel, everyone agreed, and Lou was not one to stand in the way. Now I was on the inside. I would be traveling to spring training for six weeks, then I'd make two visits to thirteen cities with the Boston Red Sox.

17

Filling The Potholes

Kate and I went to my parents' for dinner the night before I left for spring training. I took out the Clemens check and slapped it on the table in front of my brother.

"Oh, big deal, you got a check from Roger Clemens." It took a second for him to notice. "Holy...what the hell is that?"

My mother put her fork down and held her bite; my father's eyes widened.

"What? Give it to me," my father said. "You've got to be kiddin'!" He shook his head, held the check at arm's length. "No way."

"Hey, it's just a clerical error," I quipped.

"Would someone tell me what is going on?" asked my mother.

My father handed her the check.

"She'll never see it," my brother said.

"Oh, glory!" my mother exclaimed. "Scott David, why did Roger Clemens write you a check for $52,000?"

My brother and father were laughing.

"Mom, it's a mistake."

"How do you make a mistake like that?" She held the check in front of her and pointed to the box containing the dollar amount. "It's not like he added an extra zero, the comma is in the right place!"

"Mom, his wife wrote out the check," I said.

"Wouldn't you do a little proofreading before you wrote out a check for $52,000?"

"Apparently not," I said.

"He probably had a few others that day," Kevin said. "And it's tough when you only have third grade math skills."

"Shut up," I said. "You have no clue."

"I know, I know. Poor Clemens is misunderstood. And Shaughnessy's a curly-haired yard ape who doesn't know anything about baseball."

"You've been listening," I said.

My mother was too disturbed to eat. "I just don't understand how this could happen."

"Rita," said my father, "he makes 3 million a year."

She gasped, covered her mouth. "That's sick!"

"When's The Q coming back?" my brother asked over dessert. He loved Quintana and was shocked to hear of his misfortune.

"I don't know."

"What the hell happened, anyway? So he's speeding around in some car with his cousin and breaks his arm?"

"Yeah, it's terrible," I said. "They say he might be back by the All-Star break." Quintana was seriously injured in a wreck in Venezuela and would miss the entire 1992 season.

"So, we got Viola, he'll be pretty good. I remember him with the Twins. Cy Young award winner, that guy."

"Jack Clark is a bum!" my father interrupted. "The guy stands up there and whiffs half the time."

"He hit twenty-eight homers last year," I said.

"Big deal. We need someone like Teddy Ballgame. None of these guys with their 3 million dollar salaries can even come close."

"Anyway, let's talk about something a little more realistic," my brother said, rolling his eyes. "Let's get Mark McGwire! I've heard he doesn't like it in Oakland."

"The guy is hurt too much, forget it!" my father said.

I understood that most people—even my own family—didn't care that I worked for the Red Sox, that I had some knowledge and expertise. Their love for the Red Sox was personal, and they thought about the team in their own way. Everything was subjective. Everyone was their own manager during the game, and their own general manager during the winter months when trades were made and free agents were signed.

My brother and father would've enjoyed hearing some of the things I'd learned about Greenwell, Boggs, and Clemens, and while telling them would've made me a Red Sox insider, I'd have been an outsider in my own family. I had extra information; it was like cheating. Sometimes I wished I didn't know these extra things, that I could argue vehemently about the Sox, leave all logic behind and spout off in emotional bursts about how a player sucked and should be discarded.

But I knew them as people. I knew there were a lot of factors. I knew too much.

That was O.K., though. This is what I wanted, to get under the covers, to study and learn, to help the coaches, to provide critical data to a player that could affect the outcome of the game. The clowns up in Media Relations, the reporters, even the front-office staff did not affect the game. They lined up the pieces and waited for the result. I could produce critical reports that prodded players to make adjustments. I could help win games. I would live and breathe baseball for the next twelve months. Six weeks in spring training. Thirteen cities. Eighty-one road games. By the end of the season I wanted to be able to recite each American League pitcher's repertoire, name each hitter's weakness. With this information, I would help the greatest team in professional sports win its first World Series since 1918. I had it all figured out: I would be in the clubhouse in the ninth, would sneak down into the dugout for the final out, and run out onto the field to join the pile.

The Mustang was packed and ready to go. I left it in the parking lot in front of Kate's apartment, busting with two suitcases of clothes, a basketball, two bags filled with cookies, soda and chips, and a milk crate of CD's.

At 4:30 A.M. the alarm jarred me awake. I kissed Kate on the cheek, hopped in and out of the shower, and threw on jeans and my Terminator T-Shirt. In the dark chill of a New England February morning, I was smiling to myself—instantly and completely awake—dreaming of the Florida sun. With a pen from the kitchen drawer, I wrote a goodbye note to Kate. *I'll call you tonight from South Carolina, don't work too hard, see you in April.* I grabbed my coat, keys, and wallet and pulled the door shut behind me.

The wind whipped through the parking lot and I turned to greet it, let it scrape my face, freeze my nose. I slid the key into the Mustang and turned the lock, but frost held the door shut; I punched the glass with the side of my fist to break the seal. The Mustang charged to life. I would be in New York City before the morning rush hour, Baltimore around lunch time, North Carolina by dinner. By breakfast on Wednesday, February 12, I'd be in Winter Haven, Florida, checking into the Holiday Inn. Phil was already there, and he called me last night to say he'd take me to the Denny's over on Route 540, his treat.

"After breakfast I'll take you over to the yard, show you around," he had said.

"Sounds good. Hey, Phil, one last thing."

"Yeah, what?"

"Are there any special instructors there at spring training?"

"Special instructors?"

"Former Red Sox players, who come to spring training to help out."

"The old guys? Yeah, there are old guys here. The only one I knew was Yaz."

"You'd better know Yaz, you punk…"

"Got him to sign a ball for my dad. Someone showed me his numbers. Damn, that man could rake!"

"Yeah, he could." I cleared my throat. "Do you know if Jim Rice was there?"

"Rice? I don't know him. What's he look like?"

"You're pathetic. He would've been wearing number fourteen. Big guy."

"Good golfer?"

"Yes."

"Sure, he was there. Didn't say much. Kinda kept to himself."

Pause.

"Why, you know him?" Phil asked.

"No. But I used to have a T-shirt with a drawing of Jim Rice on it. Below the picture, in thick black letters it said, 'Pitchers pay the price when they face Jim Rice!'"

Phil laughed. "And you wore that?"

"I was ten, of course I wore it."

"So, if I get forty bombs this season, they'll be making shirts with my picture on it?"

"Do it for two or three years, then maybe they'll make you some shirts."

"How about 'Pitchers cry a tear when they face Plantier!'"

"Horrible."

"Screw you. Let's hear what you got."

"The pitchers shake with fear when they face Plantier!"

"Not bad."

In two months it will be time for Little League in Winchester. In a random assignment, an eight-year-old kid will get Phil's number twenty-nine, and when it's September and the Sox are battling to get to the World Series, the kid will hold his breath every time Plantier comes up.

This year Phil will come through, the Sox will win it all, and the kid with the number twenty nine jersey—when he revisits his childhood memories decades later—will find exhilaration where I found tragedy. But I will uncover perhaps a greater joy than the young boy, for when they win it all (they picked up Viola this year, a Cy Young winner, after all) it'll reshape my past and mend the potholes of disappointment with a steaming coat of shiny asphalt. It could happen, you know.

This could be the year.

1991 Boston Red Sox Team Batting

Pos	Player	Ag	G	AB	R	H	2B	3B	HR	RBI	BB	SO	BA	OBP	SLG	SB	CS
C	Tony Pena	34	141	464	45	107	23	2	5	48	37	53	.231	.291	.321	8	3
1B	Carlos Quintana	25	149	478	69	141	21	1	11	71	61	66	.295	.375	.412	1	0
2B	Jody Reed	28	153	618	87	175	42	2	5	60	60	53	.283	.349	.382	6	5
3B	*Wade Boggs	33	144	546	93	181	42	2	8	51	89	32	.332	.421	.460	1	2
SS	Luis Rivera	27	129	414	64	107	22	3	8	40	35	86	.258	.318	.384	4	4
OF	*Mike Greenwell	27	147	544	76	163	26	6	9	83	43	35	.300	.350	.419	15	5
OF	Tom Brunansky	30	142	459	54	105	24	1	16	70	49	72	.229	.303	.390	1	2
OF	Ellis Burks	26	130	474	56	119	33	3	14	56	39	81	.251	.314	.422	6	11
DH	Jack Clark	35	140	481	75	120	18	1	28	87	96	133	.249	.374	.466	0	2
	*Mo Vaughn	23	74	219	21	57	12	0	4	32	26	43	.260	.339	.370	2	1
	*Steve Lyons	31	87	212	15	51	10	1	1	17	11	35	.241	.277	.354	10	3
	*Phil Plantier	22	53	148	27	49	7	1	11	35	23	38	.331	.420	.615	1	0
	#Mike Brumley	28	63	118	16	25	5	0	0	5	10	22	.212	.273	.254	2	0
	John Marzano	28	49	114	10	30	8	0	0	9	1	16	.263	.271	.333	0	0
	Mike Marshall	31	22	62	4	18	4	0	1	7	0	19	.290	.290	.403	0	0
	Tim Naehring	24	20	55	1	6	1	0	0	3	6	15	.109	.197	.127	0	0
	Kevin Romine	30	44	55	7	9	2	0	1	7	3	10	.164	.207	.255	1	1
	*Scott Cooper	23	14	35	6	16	4	2	0	7	2	2	.457	.486	.686	0	1
	Bob Zupcic	24	18	25	3	4	0	0	1	3	1	6	.160	.192	.280	0	0
	#Wayne Housie	26	11	8	2	2	1	0	0	0	1	3	.250	.333	.375	1	0
	Eric Wedge	23	1	1	0	1	0	0	0	0	0	0	1.000	1.000	1.000	0	0
TOTAL team age - 29.0			162	5530	731	1486	305	25	126	691	593	820	.269	.340	.401	59	39
Rank among 14 AL teams					9	7	4	1	12	9	5	11	4	2	4	13	12

| | | Ag | G | AB | R | H | 2B | 3B | HR | RBI | BB | SO | BA | OBP | SLG | SB | CS |

* - bats left-handed, # - switch hits, ? - unknown, else - bats right-handed

by baseball-reference.com (Copyright ©2000-2003).

1991 Boston Red Sox Team Pitching

	Player	Ag	G	ERA	W	L	SV	GS	CG	SHO	IP	H	ER	BB	HR	SO
SP	Roger Clemens	28	35	2.62	18	10	0	35	13	4	271.3	219	79	65	15	241
SP	Mike Gardiner	25	22	4.85	9	10	0	22	0	0	130.0	140	70	47	18	91
SP	*Tom Bolton	29	25	5.24	8	9	0	19	0	0	110.0	136	64	51	16	64
SP	*Matt Young	32	19	5.18	3	7	0	16	0	0	88.7	92	51	53	4	69
SP	*Kevin Morton	22	16	4.59	6	5	0	15	1	0	86.3	93	44	40	9	45
SP	Danny Darwin	35	12	5.16	3	6	0	12	0	0	68.0	71	39	15	15	42
CL	Jeff Reardon	35	57	3.03	1	4	40	0	0	0	59.3	54	20	16	9	44
RP	*Tony Fossas	33	64	3.47	3	2	1	0	0	0	57.0	49	22	28	3	29
RP	Dennis Lamp	38	51	4.70	6	3	0	0	0	0	92.0	100	48	31	8	57
RP	Jeff Gray	28	50	2.34	2	3	1	0	0	0	61.7	39	16	10	7	41
RP	Greg Harris	35	53	3.85	11	12	2	21	1	0	173.0	157	74	69	13	127
	*Joe Hesketh	32	39	3.29	12	4	0	17	0	0	153.3	142	56	53	19	104
	Dana Kiecker	30	18	7.36	2	3	0	5	0	0	40.3	56	33	23	6	21
	Dan Petry	32	13	4.43	0	0	1	0	0	0	22.3	21	11	12	3	12
	Daryl Irvine	26	9	6.00	0	0	0	0	0	0	18.0	25	12	9	2	8
	Jeff Plympton	25	4	0.00	0	0	0	0	0	0	5.3	5	0	4	0	2
	John Dopson	27	1	18.00	0	0	0	0	0	0	1.0	2	2	1	0	0
	Steve Lyons	31	1	0.00	0	0	0	0	0	0	1.0	2	0	0	0	1
	Josias Manzanillo	23	1	18.00	0	0	0	0	0	0	1.0	2	2	3	0	1
	TOTAL team age – 30.8		162	4.01	84	78	45	162	15	13	1439.0	1405	641	530	147	999
	Rank among 14 AL teams			7	5	8	6	8	2	14	9	7		6		4
		Ag	G	ERA	W	L	SV	GS	CG	SHO	IP	H	ER	BB	HR	SO

baseball-reference.com (Copyright ©2000-2003).

1991 Boston Red Sox Salaries

Player	Salary		Player	Salary
Danny Darwin	$ 3,250,000		John Dopson	$ 265,000
Jack Clark	$ 2,900,000		Dana Kiecker	$ 167,500
Wade Boggs	$ 2,750,000		Tony Fossas	$ 165,000
Roger Clemens	$ 2,700,000		Jeff Gray	$ 155,000
Mike Greenwell	$ 2,650,000		Tim Naehring	$ 125,000
Jeff Reardon	$ 2,533,333		John Marzano	$ 105,000
Tom Brunansky	$ 2,500,000		Scott Cooper	$ 100,000
Tony Pena	$ 2,300,000		Mo Vaughn	$ 100,000
Matt Young	$ 2,266,667		Bob Zupcic	$ 100,000
Ellis Burks	$ 1,825,000			
Greg Harris	$ 1,300,000		baseball-reference.com (Copyright ©2000-2003).	
Mike Marshall	$ 1,300,000			
Jody Reed	$ 850,000			
Dennis Lamp	$ 750,000			
Steve Lyons	$ 650,000			
Dan Petry	$ 650,000			
Luis Rivera	$ 635,000			
Joe Hesketh	$ 525,000			
Kevin Romine	$ 355,000			
Carlos Quintana	$ 305,000			
Tom Bolton	$ 290,000			

0-595-29563-0